BEYOND THE HORIZON

Beyond the
Horizon

The true story of a remarkable
young missionary in Africa

Anthea Parsons

Hodder & Stoughton

LONDON SYDNEY AUCKLAND

Line drawings by Jimmy Sonko, Julius Wegoye
and Chris Busingye

10 9 8 7 6 5 4 3 2 1

British Library Cataloguing in Publication Data
A record for this book is available from the British Library

ISBN 0 340 70989 8

Typeset by Avon Dataset Ltd, Bidford-on-Avon, Warks

Printed and bound in Great Britain by
Clays Ltd, St Ives plc

Hodder and Stoughton Ltd
A Division of Hodder Headline PLC
338 Euston Road
London NW1 3BH

To Colin
who believed in me in Christ
and Christ in me

Contents

Acknowledgments

Many thanks to Sheila Katorobo who helped me on the last stages of writing, by streamlining sections of the book. And thanks also to dear Johnson for all his prayer support, when the Ugandan electricity kept going off and putting my computer out of action.

Foreword

Anthea Parsons is a remarkable young woman, and yet she would see herself as quite ordinary. Her book, *Beyond the Horizon*, is the account of an ordinary person doing what, for many, would be considered decidedly extraordinary things!

A young, single, white woman in black Africa, often travelling alone to remote areas, is unusual enough. She has often faced danger, with only her faith in God to support her, constantly in need of His protection and provision. She has had to be bold in preaching the gospel, and has seen a steady stream of signs and wonders following her ministry, many of which are recorded here.

This book reads like an adventure story, one incident following fast upon another. It is easy to read and will stimulate your faith, for as Anthea rightly points out, Jesus is the same whenever people put their trust and confidence in Him. It is a record of God's faithfulness to her as she has obeyed His call to go and preach in His name, to love the African people with His love. Because she writes so vividly, you will find that Anthea brings Africa to life for you, and that you are sharing in her exploits, and also her experience of the drama and cost of such a ministry.

I well remember the day when Anthea came to my office and said: 'Colin, while I have been your secretary God has filled me with so much that I have to go and give it away to

others: I have to go to Africa and preach.' That is precisely
what she has done, and many thousands have been touched
with the truth of Jesus Christ and His love through Anthea.

When she was inputting my books on to her word processor,
I little expected that I would be writing the introduction to her
first book a few years later. But in that time she has been there
and done what others only dream of.

My prayer is that this is only volume one of her testimony.
Anthea is only thirty years old, with many years ahead to serve
the Lord. Many more adventures await her in Africa where
she has now made her home permanently.

And I trust that many adventures of faith await you, the
reader. For the supernatural presence and power of Jesus is
available to you, as to Anthea.

Colin Urquhart
Director, Kingdom Faith Ministries

Introduction

I sincerely hope that you enjoy following the footsteps of my last six years of missionary work in Africa. When people hear about the miracles which take place, they often say, 'Ah, but that's Africa.' In recent years, I have discovered that Jesus Christ is the same in any continent and will do the same things wherever people are ready to receive Him. I pray that this story will inspire you and that you will be encouraged to follow the instructions of Mary, the mother of Jesus when she told the servants at the wedding, 'Whatever, he says to you, do it' (John 2:5 NKJ).

> Jesus came to them and said, '. . . Go and make disciples of all nations, baptising them in the name of the Father and of the Son and of the Holy Spirit, and teaching them to obey everything I have commanded you. And surely I am with you always, to the very end of the age.' (Matt. 28:19–20)

> He told them, 'The harvest is plentiful but the workers are few. Ask the Lord of the harvest, therefore, to send out workers into his harvest field. Go! I am sending you out like lambs among wolves. (Luke 10:2–3)

1

The Days of Small Beginnings

If you are right with God, God is right with you

'What am I doing here?' I wondered, standing at the mouth of the mine surrounded by Tanzanian men of different tribes. There were no other white people for miles in this sandy desert land. I had armed guards for protection.

'Women aren't allowed down the mine,' someone said, so I went to buy a drink in a wooden shack to relieve my disappointment and my dehydration! After preaching in a newly built church, I waited for our driver to repair the punctured Land Rover tyre. I sat beside a row of Masai men, a warrior tribe in traditional dress; their tall, lean figures covered by a red cloth draped over one shoulder, a spear in the left hand, loopy earlobes dangling and beaded jewellery round the ankles and neck.

Johnson leaned over my shoulder: 'Why don't you preach to them?'

'No way!' I thought.

'Yes you will,' said the Holy Spirit.

I beckoned to my interpreter and stood before the captive audience, taking a deep breath before starting. A small group of men listened intently as the good news of Jesus touched their hearts. Suddenly a shout was heard outside – maybe someone had found a large piece of tanzanite, the blue-purple stone mined only in Tanzania. Eleven Masai men ran out of the hut, leaving me speaking to the remaining five.

I looked at one man sitting on a bench. In an instant, God gave me supernatural knowledge about him.

'Do you have a bad knee?' I asked, pointing to his right knee. Everyone nodded, obviously aware of the problem.

'Can I pray for you? Jesus wants to heal you,' I told the man.

With a little persuasion from his friends, he agreed. I placed my hand on his knee and prayed; the knee-cap moved about under the palm of my hand. He stood up, instantly healed, shouting loudly. He began jumping up and down in traditional Masai style. Immediately, the others rushed back into the hut to see what was happening.

'You see, what I'm telling you is true! Jesus is alive!' I told them. Some knelt on the dirt floor, spear in hand, giving their lives to Jesus Christ.

'How did you get into this?' people often ask. Here is the story.

* * *

3

At the age of nine I first discovered Jesus was real. In 1977 at a Bible camp, I saw children of my own age worshipping the Lord with their hands raised in the air and a peaceful expression on their faces. Sometimes a child would come to the front with a word from God concerning another child. They would pray for one another and immediate answers often occurred. I saw things I'd never seen before.

I made two little friends from the city of Bath.

'Do you know Jesus as your personal Saviour?' they asked me.

'What do you mean?' I questioned, not understanding the terminology.

'Oh, that means you don't,' they concluded. 'Have you received the Holy Spirit? Do you speak in tongues?'

It didn't make sense to me, so they took me round the back of a building.

'We're going to pray in tongues, but we're not doing it to show off. We're just speaking to God,' they explained.

That week, I watched from a distance, without fully embracing what I saw. However, the Lord healed me of terrible migraine headaches which had become more and more frequent.

A year or two later at the Downs Bible Week I started to understand for myself what a personal relationship with Jesus was about. In the children's meetings we were taught about the baptism of the Holy Spirit. I watched as boys and girls spoke in tongues, tears of joy streaming down their faces. I also received the Holy Spirit, but in a very peaceful manner. God spoke to my heart: 'I have chosen you!' From that time on, I knew I was important to God.

The theme scripture for the week was: 'Do not conform any longer to the pattern of this world, but be transformed by the renewing of your mind' (Rom. 12:2). The teaching had a profound effect on my life. I didn't attempt to taste the empty things of the world, despite the persecution I suffered at school for being so different.

I reasoned that if God just wanted me to have a happy time, He would have taken me up to heaven as soon as I was born again. So He must have a purpose for me down here. I determined to let my short life count for something in God's eyes. 'Lord, use me to bring others to You,' was my prayer.

As a family we moved to a different church. During the time we were there, it grew from a few elderly people to a thriving community. Mum and Dad were very involved, running Sunday school and a youth group, and teaching new believers. In the same house group there were solicitors, school teachers, ex-convicts and alcoholics, street sweepers, students and grannies. We had freedom to contribute during worship, in prophetic songs, words of knowledge and praying for the sick and oppressed.

In 1984, I studied for A levels and the Private Secretary's Certificate at Crawley College of Technology. In my second year, the Christian Union met in a classroom instead of a cupboard! A slender, blond-haired young man called Ralph Witherall waltzed into the room. 'There's sin in this college, and if we don't shine the light of Jesus, no one else will. We've got to pray and pray and pray without ceasing,' he urged. 'I know what I'm aiming at while I'm here and if any of you want to do the same, you can.'

We experienced some unusual things in those classrooms, as the power of God touched people and many were filled with His Spirit. Sometimes two people started singing the same song simultaneously, led by the Holy Spirit. Evangelism and revival became my heartbeat, and a lifestyle of prayer and fasting developed. I wanted to see God at work in Horsham, my home town, saving many people.

'Why don't we get together one evening and praise the Lord?' suggested Ralph. We packed out someone's lounge with Christian Union members from Crawley, Horsham and Haywards Heath. Ralph played his guitar and we rejoiced before God for an hour and worshipped Him. What happened can only be described as a sovereign move of God. He visited us, healing us physically and emotionally. Once, a demon manifested, catching us unaware.

'Let's just do what Jesus did,' someone suggested. 'He cast them out with a word, so who's going to do it?' We were all novices learning together.

Word spread about what God was doing and we made a habit of meeting together. The lounge meetings grew in number, so we hired a church hall and organised monthly meetings called Praise Parties. We called ourselves Praise with a Vision and ten of us met regularly each week to pray for the coming Praise Party. We wrote down what the Lord showed us about the people who would come.

One time, Geoff, a member of our team, phoned to say he couldn't attend. He'd been in bed for a couple of days with a bad leg, unable to move. 'We're going to pray for you right now, Geoff. Stand by for your healing,' Jon said, replacing the receiver. We prayed together intensely until we sensed a breakthrough. At that moment the telephone rang again. It was Geoff: 'I'm healed! I'm healed!' God was at work.

Our emphasis was on unity. When the disciples were in one accord, the Holy Spirit was out-poured, so we made every effort to keep love and peace flowing between us. We prayed for an hour together before each Praise Party. On one occasion things were not taking off. We stopped to find out why. It transpired that one member was experiencing some personal problems. We gathered round him lovingly and prayed and prophesied until he was free. God was able to move and we went out into the main meeting, full of the Holy Spirit, with joy and faith.

After praising for an hour or more, the team would pray with people. Anything could have happened. We waited on God for His direction. In one Praise Party we split into two groups and went into different rooms. Our group sat in a circle listening to the Lord to see what He wanted to do.

'I think He wants to give us joy,' someone said.

'That's what I sensed!' shouted another.

So we asked the Holy Spirit to come and do His work, and all heaven was let loose. We had never experienced anything like it. By the time the others came in, bodies littered the floor. In that meeting, God did something so deep in my life, I was never the same again. He set me apart and released me from the inferiority complex that had plagued me. People were amazed that the oldest among us was only seventeen. What we experienced was beyond anything we'd seen in our churches. This move of God lasted for a year before we scattered to go to university and various other places.

When I started work, the office became my mission field. My first job started as two days' temporary work. I sensed an urgency to tell people about Jesus, in case they had no other chance to hear the good news. God opened up natural opportunities for me to share the love of Christ and I was offered full-time employment, which I accepted. Before going to work, I would read my Bible and pray, asking God to fill me with the Holy Spirit.

'Why are you always happy?' several people asked.

While typing on the computer, I kept my spirit in tune

with God, praying in tongues behind closed lips so that no one thought I was mad. I was ready for opportunities; at the photocopier, in the canteen and in the ladies' toilets. Sometimes after work, I spent hours explaining the gospel to genuine inquirers. I never wasted time with argumentative people or with those who were not open to listen.

I had a great conversation with a young, blonde accountant called Sam. I explained what it meant to be born again.

'I don't want to pray here, but I'll do it in private tonight,' she said.

I went home excited. The next day by mid-morning she was not at her desk.

'Where's Sam?' I asked the others in her department.

'Oh, she got the sack,' they replied.

'What for? When?'

'It must have been at the end of work, but we don't know why; it was the manager's decision.'

I had no way of contacting her, but I prayed, placing her in the Lord's hands.

One day a lady in the next department gave me great encouragement.

'Ever since you've been working here, the whole atmosphere has changed,' she told me.

'That's because God is with me,' I answered.

The light was dispelling the darkness in that place. I once became so fed up with a young man's obscenities, I prayed at home. The words came out of my mouth, 'I bind you, spirit of lust.' After that, there was not even a whisper or a wrong look from him.

During the next few months, a Jehovah's Witness called Ruth started to soften to my words. I gave her a list of scriptures to look up. 'Do you have a personal relationship with Jesus?' I asked her. 'What has He done for you? I know what He's done for me. He saved me from my sins, He healed me and has answered so many prayers. He speaks to me every day.'

After reading the scriptures, she came back saying how touched she'd been. She wanted further discussions. But the next day, she wasn't at work. 'What's up with Ruth?' I asked, 'Is she off sick?'

'No, she got the sack,' I was told.

'Just suddenly like that?' I asked in amazement, wondering how this could happen yet again.

A few months later, I sat in the canteen next to a man who fired questions at me. I couldn't speak fast enough to give him what he wanted to hear.

'You know, my landlord is a believer like you,' he told me. 'When I get home tonight, I'm going to tell him about you and everything we've been discussing. He'll be over the moon when he hears I want to become a Christian.'

'We could pray here, you know,' I suggested, not wanting to sound pushy.

'Well, let me pray at home. I'd be happier that way.'

'OK,' I said, satisfied that I'd explained the gospel in enough depth.

You'll never guess what. That afternoon . . . he got the sack, for no apparent reason. A spiritual battle was raging in that office. The fight for people's souls was intense.

After almost a year in that company, I left and joined a temping agency. 'Lord, liaise with the agencies and put me with the people who are ready to receive Your Word,' I prayed. And God did just that. I had many adventures sharing the gospel with managers, secretaries, air hostesses, cleaners and others who were being drawn to the light of Jesus.

In this season, I had such a yearning for the presence of God. During one two-week period, I sensed God wanted to tell me something, so I spent my spare time praying, to give Him the opportunity. I sensed I needed to move on, both spiritually and geographically. 'Lord, just speak to me,' I prayed in earnest. 'Whatever it is, wherever it is, Lord, I just want to be in Your perfect will.'

I had a built-in sense of destiny. I knew that God had prepared works in advance for me to do, and somehow my spirit became aware that God was sending me to Africa. Even today, I can't explain how He spoke. That weekend, a visiting team came to my church and God moved powerfully on me. I found myself in conversation with Him. I saw the cross of Jesus, and what He did for me. I was challenged to take up my cross and follow Him. 'Are you willing? Are you really willing?' He questioned.

I knew God's plan for my life was the best. His perfect love would ensure the right choice for me. I opened my eyes and saw one of the visitors praying beside me.

'Is God showing you anything?' I asked. He seemed afraid to speak. 'Just say it, even if it's big. I'll test it.'

'As soon as I came into this church, I saw a banner over you with AFRICA written on it,' he told me.

The words hit my heart like an arrow. Convinced now that the idea was not some wild imagination, I said, 'Lord, I'll go, but what is Africa?' I had read no books about Africa, I'd never met an African and I knew very little about that massive continent.

For the next three weeks, everything revolved around Africa. The following Sunday, a young Ugandan pastor turned up at our church. He later stayed for seven months at my parents' house. The next week, the youth group went to see a film, set in South Africa. Then we had a visiting speaker in church who had been to Malawi; he showed slides and spoke about his trip. Next I was placed in a new job and met a lady who'd recently been born again in South Africa. Everywhere I looked it was Africa, Africa, Africa. I was so happy, taken up with God, but I didn't breathe a word to anyone, although I was prepared to pack my bags and go at any moment.

Coming from a Christian family was a definite advantage. When I was about twelve my mum said, 'You belong more to God than you do to me and Dad,' and I was free to do whatever God wanted.

I planned to spend three months at Roffey Place Christian Training Centre as a student. It was a mile away from my parents' home. While still temping, I saved my money to pay the fees. If I worked every week up to the time I left for Roffey Place, I would have enough money. However, one Monday I came down with flu symptoms. When I became ill, normally I would spend the morning praying and by the afternoon I would be at work again, healed by the presence and power of Jesus Christ. However, this time by Wednesday I was still in bed. I felt restless and after a while I realised that I was worried about the money. Where would I get a week's wages from? The Lord ministered to me and the Holy Spirit did His convicting work.

'Forgive me, Lord,' I sobbed. 'I've been trusting in my own ability instead of looking to You as my only source of supply. From now on I will look to You only as my Provider.'

The following week I received a letter from my friend David, who had just left his job to join full-time ministry. 'I don't understand why, but God told me to send you this,' he wrote. Inside was a cheque for the sum of a week's wages, dated the day I repented of my unbelief.

My time at Roffey Place was both refreshing and challenging. I enjoyed the evangelism trips with the King's Coaches. I stayed for two terms as a student and ended up becoming a member of Colin Urquhart's team. I was surprised God didn't send me to Africa immediately, as I had such a sense of urgency, but He kept me waiting. He had spoken earlier about Africa to show me what I was being trained for. 'I'm building a foundation in your life of love and prayer,' the Holy Spirit told me.

After a few months I started to travel with Colin and became his secretary. Words cannot express what God did during this three-year period to prepare me for what lay ahead. I gained a fresh understanding of the Word of God and my relationship with Jesus was strengthened. I grew confident in hearing God and stepping out in obedience.

One day, while I was sorting out the student application forms for Roffey Place, the passport photo of a blonde-haired young lady caught my eye. She was working as a missionary in Spain. 'She'll be very important to you. She's going to be a good friend,' the Holy Spirit told me. When Jan Marchant was accepted as a student in the college, I made a point of saying hello to her, but it was not until the mission to Scotland that we became good friends. A minibus-load of students came for two weeks. When they returned to Roffey, Jan filled the space in our car for the next week's mission.

We shared a room in the house of a Christian family. My bed was uncomfortable so on the second night I decided to sleep on the floor.

'Oh, I'm so glad you've done that,' said Jan, pulling the duvet off her narrow bed. 'I wasn't comfortable either. I often get fed up with beds and sleep on the floor anyway,' she told me openly. We discovered that we enjoyed doing the same sort of crazy things, like swimming under the stars at 10.00 at night, and had a similar sense of humour.

Colin, Guy, Jan and I stayed in a hotel for a break. In the morning, I walked around the lake. The Lord told me,

'Get ready to receive some encouragement today.'

Back in the room Jan was sprawled out over the bed, her Bible open. 'You know what,' she said, 'God doesn't usually speak to me like this, but He's told me to stand with you and that He's uniting us like David and Jonathan. Their souls were knitted together and Jonathan loved David as himself. He even gave David his sword. And this is what God is telling me to do for you.' I was amazed and delighted. From that time on, before I went on a mission, Jan prayed with me and wrote out a key scripture for the trip. She always knew how things were going while I was away. She was a great support and a fun friend.

Her lifestyle of faith was a great encouragement to me. One morning, Jan discovered she had no toothpaste left and no money to buy another tube. She prayed and the answer came very swiftly. As she checked her post downstairs she found a parcel from her friend in America. Inside was a giant-sized tube of her favourite toothpaste.

One day a letter arrived inviting Colin to Nigeria. 'I don't suppose you would be interested in coming, would you?' he joked. He knew about my heart for Africa.

The night before we left for Nigeria, my mind raced with a thousand thoughts. I hardly slept. The next day I boarded the plane, not quite believing we were really going. Jonathan Croft and I had already obtained visas, but Colin had come across some obstacles. He had felt the Lord was telling us not to go on that particular flight, but the Nigerians assured him on the phone that everything would be all right. They would arrange for someone to collect us from the airport and get us through Immigration.

Having travelled non-stop for weeks, I was extremely tired, but also excited about what lay ahead. As the wheels touched the runway at Lagos Airport, the voice of the

Holy Spirit took me by surprise: 'Welcome home,' He said.

Jonathan and I were checked through Immigration and waited for Colin. After a few minutes, he was escorted into another office. He appeared again and quickly explained that he was being sent back to England on the next plane. He thrust some dollars into Jonathan's hands saying, 'I'll try to come back.' Then he was whisked away out of sight. We collected our luggage and wondered what to do next. No one had come to meet us. In the rush we hadn't even asked Colin for the contact address. All I knew was the name of the ministry, because of the letter I'd typed accepting the invitation.

'If ever I needed your peace, Lord, I need it now,' I prayed.

Here we were, in a foreign country, sitting on the floor in Lagos Airport, surrounded by people. For both of us, this was our first time of setting foot on African soil.

I left Jonathan with the luggage and approached people who seemed to be looking for someone. 'Are you with Sword of the Spirit Ministries?' I asked, but the reply was always negative. After half an hour, I sat on my suitcase next to Jonathan.

'Well, what do we do now? Lord, what do we do?'

Just then, a man came walking directly up to us.

'Hello, I'm a friend of Francis Wale Oke's. He asked me to check on you here. I'm about to fly to Ghana to see my wife,' the man told us. We explained the situation to him. 'You need some help,' he said. 'Wait here while I cancel my flight.'

He soon returned and we followed him outside, carrying our suitcases. By this time it was dark. The hot, humid air almost clung to my face. An unusual smell hung in the atmosphere.

The man opened the boot of his blue VW Beetle. It

was full of water melons so we put the suitcases on the back seat and I sat on Jonathan's lap in the front. 'It's not far,' he assured us.

We arrived at the Stop-Over Motel and booked two rooms for the night. Our newly acquired friend expected to share a double bed with Jonathan.

'I'll sleep on the floor,' Jonathan insisted. But the man slept on the floor himself, when he realised Jonathan was serious.

I had been in the country for only an hour and was already dripping with sweat. In my room, the stench from the last person was still lingering on the bed sheets. I switched on the air-conditioning unit attached to the side of the wall. It made a noisy, clanky sound but I guessed it would cool the room down and I could switch it off before I went to sleep. However, it seemed that none of the dials could turn it off. I tried to sleep through the noise. It soon became extremely cold so I put on several layers of the summer clothes I had packed. Morning dawned at last, but I hadn't managed to sleep at all. There was a knock on my door. I opened it to find Jonathan standing there singing 'Happy Birthday', holding a bottle of bubble bath in his hand. How far removed this was from our situation.

'Did you sleep?' I asked.

'No,' he replied, 'that man snored all night.'

'I didn't sleep either. This rattling air-conditioning unit kept me awake. I couldn't turn it off and I was frozen – yet this is Africa!'

We started to laugh and then prayed, committing everything into the Lord's hands.

As we left the room, I noticed that the cleaners were singing praises to God openly as they went about their work. The face of the receptionist shone with the glory of God.

'Is this a Christian hotel?' I asked our host.

'No, but there are many Christians working here,' he replied.

When I had prayed for revival in my home town, I envisaged the Christians there being bold like this as they went about their everyday lives. Maybe this was a touch of revival. Did they really say that 40 per cent of Lagos's population was born again?

After breakfast, our kind host put us into a taxi and we travelled for two hours to Ibadan. Despite the exhaustion, I forced my eyelids to stay open so I wouldn't miss the amazing sights. The thick vegetation was unusually green, not at all how I had imagined Africa to be. Many people walked along the dusty roadside: children in brightly coloured school uniforms and women carrying great loads. I saw someone with a typewriter on her head. A man sat up to a desk typing under the shade of a sheet of cardboard, while the traffic passed by. A sign could be clearly seen: 'Secretarial Services'.

Finally we arrived at the ministry headquarters and I met Francis Wale Oke for the first time. He seemed a very gracious man, full of the Holy Spirit. He was not aware of what had happened to Colin, and had been expecting to meet us in the Sheraton Hotel in Lagos. We were due to fly to Abuja, Nigeria's new federal capital. We stayed in his office for twenty minutes before getting another taxi back to Lagos.

'Hey, this car's got a hole,' I told Jonathan, pointing to the rusty floor and watching as the road whizzed past my foot. By the time we arrived back at the airport, we had missed the plane, so we waited in the airport lounge for five hours for the next one, eating fried chicken to relieve the hunger and the boredom.

Francis had asked us if we were ready to preach in the

conference. I explained that I had come to support Colin in prayer. I wasn't going to preach, if I could help it. Once, I had said to Colin, 'You'll never get me preaching. I'm a one-to-one person.' He had looked at me with an expression on his face which said he knew something I didn't.

The twenty-seater plane arrived. We flew for an hour over areas of hard-baked mud and small villages with round, thatched huts. We really were in Africa. On landing, we were driven to a hotel and taken straight into the meeting hall. I was astonished to see a very high platform on which was a long table with a white cloth. About five hundred people, wearing brightly coloured clothes, sang and swayed in time to the music. We were directed on to the stage.

'I can't sit up there in front of everyone. Let me stay down here with the people,' I protested, But they wouldn't allow it. I had to take the place of honour.

I observed my surroundings. Things were different, yet something seemed strangely familiar. The presence of God made me feel instantly at home. The Nigerians had a large concept of God – I sensed the power in the atmosphere as people sang. Then the preaching began. It was good, but I felt weary trying to stay composed in front of all the people. When the third preacher was introduced, I discreetly asked permission to go back to the hotel room to sleep.

The next day I was asked to speak to some church leaders, for which I was totally unprepared. The theme I chose was the importance of love as the foundation and motivation for all Christian activity. I stood up and looked at the people, and my eyes were drawn to a man with a terrible expression of disapproval on his face. Fear filled my heart as I stuttered my first words, and the man stood up and left the room. I managed to read a few scriptures and sat down quickly. The co-ordinator of the meeting read from Hebrews: 'Do not throw away your confidence. In the end it will be richly rewarded.' I took this as a great encouragement.

For the first three days in Nigeria I struggled with feelings of spiritual inferiority in the light of the vibrant faith which was being displayed all around me. I had considered myself to be quite a strong Christian in England, yet it was as if I hadn't begun to walk with the Lord. He had done many things in my life, yet I felt I hardly knew Him. It was humbling to face my spiritual barrenness. I was often close to tears, but managed to bottle it up inside me in true English fashion! If God was to use me in Africa in the future, I would need Him in my life in a greater way than ever before.

I heard testimonies of miracles and breakthroughs in the face of much opposition and suffering. There was a strong Muslim influence everywhere and new mosques were being constructed. One Christian said, 'We're not worried about that. These buildings will soon be used as churches.'

Another story we heard was about an open-air meeting. The Christians set up a stage and placed stadium-type seats all around. The night before the crusade, some Muslims burnt everything, having sought permission from a well-known authority in the government. The Christians prayed fervently in the open ground. That night the government minister died unexpectedly and the fear of God came into the town. Many put their faith in Jesus Christ as a result.

We returned to Ibadan and stayed in a hotel for three days while Colin's visa was being worked on. I took this as an opportunity to seek God, but Jonathan seemed restless. He was due to be married in six weeks' time and was missing Helena. He suggested we should return to England.

'No way,' I thought to myself. 'I'm here in Africa at last; nothing can send me back home early.'

I prayed for Colin to get his visa and sensed he would be joining us soon. I read in my Bible: 'With your own eyes, you shall see your teacher.' That was enough confirmation for me. Francis Wale Oke was always positive. 'Don't be afraid; we are more than conquerors,' he said. 'The devil has been fighting, but when Colin comes, we'll hit the enemy so hard.' And within a few days we collected Colin from the airport.

We travelled to Abeokuta. I had never before sat in front of thousands of people who had come to hear the gospel. Seeing them surrendering their lives to the Lord en masse was quite an experience. In every city, thousands responded. I was impressed by the way the Nigerians organised the follow-up. After we left, they conducted a week of teaching for the new believers, praying with each one individually. At first I had wondered how genuine these conversions were, but I became convinced that this was thorough, effective, large-scale evangelism. In Western civilisation, we are very individualistic and I believe this is expressed to some degree in our Christianity. Sometimes in Africa a whole community or village can come to the Lord in true repentance.

I came back from Africa with a seed of faith deposited in my heart. I didn't speak much about what I had experienced, but the vision had been birthed in my spirit, and my call to Africa confirmed.

2

God is a Refuge

Receiving love does not make you more selfish;
it makes you more loving

I lay in my room thinking. I had just left the Kingdom
Faith team. It was strange trying to return to what most
people would consider to be normal life. What was normal
anyway? Was it normal to do what was expected of a
twenty-three-year-old, or to follow closely to the Creator's
instructions? I knew my life could not just settle down into
a routine. God had promised that by the end of the year I
would be in Africa. How that would happen, I did not know.

After temping as a secretary for a few weeks, I went to Faith '91, a camp run by Kingdom Faith. Five thousand people stayed in tents and caravans for a week, seeking the Lord, receiving good teaching and enjoying fellowship with other Christians. Walking through the field having eaten a delicious lunch, I saw Colin coming directly towards me.

'I've just been with David Ndarahutse. He needs an English-speaking secretary. How about it?'

David originated in Rwanda, but had lived most of his life in Uganda. He was a Roffey student in the mid-1980s, after which he started a work in Burundi, central Africa, called African Revival Ministries (ARM). He had kept contact with everyone at Kingdom Faith and was one of the seminar speakers at the camp. I spoke to David for ten minutes, by the end of which I had decided to go to Burundi for a few months. God had opened the door.

The heat hit me as I walked down the steps of the plane and across the tarmac into the airport building.

'Hello! Anthea!' a voice called.

I looked up and saw David leaning over the banister at the top of a spiral staircase. His presence was reassuring. I put my French to immediate use explaining to the man at Immigration that David was there to sort out my visa.

David was born in Rwanda. At the tender age of five, he saw his father shot before his eyes. He and his young brothers and sisters escaped to Uganda, walking cross-country for two years, narrowly escaping death from wild animals and a near-accident while crossing a river. Although he grew up in a refugee camp, he graduated from Makerere University. God called him to Burundi where he soon became secretary to the archbishop over-seeing the Anglican churches of Burundi, Rwanda and

21

part of Zaïre. While he was attending Roffey Place with his wife Ruth and their first son, Peter, God gave him a vision, which he set about implementing on his return to Burundi. Misunderstood by other churches, they lived up-country for a couple of years to establish the Bible College before moving down into the city. I felt privileged to stand with such a man of God.

David and Ruth's house was always packed with people, but they gave me a room to myself. In it was a double bed, a desk, a chair and a cupboard where I hung up my six outfits suitable for the tropical heat. From the bedroom window through the mosquito netting I could see Lake Tanganyika glistening in the distance, where hippos often wallowed, yawning widely at dusk.

I soon got used to the food. It was starchy but really pleasant. Rice was quite common and we also ate a variety of bananas cooked in different ways. Bright yellow savoury ones were mashed with spinach or carrots. Some were cooked whole, and one sweet variety was sliced and deep fried. They were my favourite. We ate tasty peanut sauce and eggs from the chickens kept down at the bottom of the garden. We didn't eat much meat, but often had tiny silver fish called *ndagara* which were about two inches long, freshly caught from the lake and cooked in real tomato sauce.

David drove me up the mountain to Sororezo where Chrissie Chapman was running a maternity clinic. I had met her when she was assisting Bob Gordon at Roffey Place. She had seen God's miraculous provision in order to serve the ever-expanding local population. Women would sometimes walk for miles to have their babies at the clinic, resting for a few hours on a bed before strapping the new-born baby to their backs and starting the long journey home. The government built a road to the clinic which benefited the whole community, but water still had to be carried up in jerricans by car from the city, until one evening Chrissie spotted the president's wife jogging past her house. She invited her in for a cup of tea – and within a few months, men were sent to dig trenches for the waterpipes.

Close to the clinic was a healing centre. Periodically, David and his nephew, Edmond, would collect mentally handicapped people from the lakeside, loading them into the minibus. They were found wandering about naked, completely out of their minds. They stayed in the healing centre and were occasionally taken to the Bible College at Nyakarago where the atmosphere of praise and worship worked wonders among them. Then, after fasting and private prayer, David would pray with them and cast out demons. I spoke to one girl who had returned to school after five years of wandering in the streets. 'Jesus, my Saviour, has rescued me,' she said with a wide smile.

For an office ARM rented a house in town. I sat down to type on the computer, but it was unusable. All the keys stuck together. The only way to use it was to punch each key down separately and pull it up quickly with a finger and thumb before a line of letters appeared on the screen. I waited a whole day while someone fetched a screwdriver. Then I took the keyboard apart and oiled each spring with massage oil, which seemed to solve the problem.

It was good to get my teeth into something, as the pace of life in Burundi was slow. David had many letters to write.

'What's that?' he asked, staring at my shorthand. 'Oh, I thought it was Arabic,' he said after I had explained.

'You can speak faster. I'll keep up with you,' I said. But he kept waiting, fascinated to see what I was writing.

'What's that word?' he asked, pointing to the outline.

'That's "ministry",' I replied.

He dictated several letters including a newsletter and I typed out a mailing list of 115 names and addresses. The newsletter had to be printed off the computer 115 times as there was no photocopier. The printer was very slow and could not hold the paper properly so Thérèse, David's French-speaking secretary, improvised by unwinding paper clips and fixing them to hold the bar down. Every now and again, it slipped and we had to reprint the sheet of paper. It took a whole hour to print the first six copies! Perseverance and patience were certainly needed.

Isn't it strange how frustrations stick in one's mind? I remember typing a booklet in Kirundi, the main language used in Burundi. After three days' hard work, the electricity cut out during a violent thunderstorm. The document was completely wiped off the computer and could not be found in the memory, so I had to start all over again.

Apart from working with ARM, I became involved in the English-speaking International Fellowship, an organisation which started years ago when different missionaries came together for prayer and encouragement. By the time I joined, it was headed by Graham and Sarah White and their five boys, who I would describe as the hub of a very caring community. Whenever a new foreigner entered the country, they would be invited to the fellowship or for a meal. I taught a group in the Sunday school, sang in the worship team and attended the women's Bible study.

My social life certainly took off. If I wasn't eating peppered steak sitting on the balcony of Les's beautiful house (which he named 'shack on the hill') overlooking the city and the lake, I could be at Lea and Jamie's house cutting people's hair. Or perhaps I would be joining in the Johnson family's devotions, having eaten American pancakes and home-made fruit ice-cream. I hiked in the mountains with Rob and Helen and swam in Lake Tanganyika, despite hearing of a woman who was snapped up in the shallows by a crocodile.

Sometimes I was given lifts to various activities by Ken, a rough-looking, bearded, sun-tanned bachelor (now married) who went around on an ancient Russian motor-bike. I would sit in the side-car, covering myself with a waterproof cape and putting on sunglasses, even in the dark, to protect my eyes from the insects. The bike could be started only by pushing, which added to the novelty of it all. Ken was an amazing character with a great sense of humour that kept me going. He often visited members of the fellowship, distributing yoghurts he had bought, or night lilies which bloom once at midnight.

Life was full of variety. After working in the office all day I would swim in next-door's pool, at the home of an American in charge of the American cultural centre. He told his house guards to let me swim any time I wanted. On another occasion, I spent a whole afternoon playing with chimpanzees at a 'sanctuary' together with the Whites and their au pair, Rachel. At first I didn't know how to relate to these animals. They looked so human with their little hands and fingernails and funny facial expressions. One cheeky chimp pulled my hairband off and went running away, squawking in delight. Another tried to do up Rachel's shoe laces. It required so much concentration to thread the lace through the hole. They were very affectionate and one kept kissing my hand. All of them had been taken out of the wild and sold to people who mistakenly thought they would make good pets. Now they could not adapt back to the wild so they needed to be looked after.

Ken and I took two of the White boys and one of Ken's

nephews on a bike ride. We cycled for miles along the flat road by the edge of the lake and stopped at a beach to swim. Cycling off again, I became aware of the presence of evil and started to pray. We went past a parked lorry loaded with sacks. There were some young men on top, throwing things down to those below. Ken was in front, with the boys following, and I cycled behind. One man brought down his arm swiftly, pointing to one of the boys as he passed. The bike went out of control and off the road, narrowly missing some people sitting outside their houses. Daniel hurt his leg, but not too severely. The men on the lorry sniggered as we cycled away. I had been aware of curses, but this incident showed me their reality.

One afternoon, I went to a hotel swimming-pool with Stella, a new-found Ugandan friend who lived with David and Ruth. After a refreshing swim we walked back along the lakeside. We were so engrossed in our conversation, I didn't even notice the young man coming up behind me. Suddenly some strong hands pinned my arms to my sides. 'What on earth is going on?' I thought, then quickly understood as another lad grabbed my bum-bag and pulled. 'In the name of Jesus!' I shouted.

The strap broke and they ran as fast as their legs could take them into the nearby banana plantation. Stella and I wondered what to do. I felt the Lord's peace surrounding me.

Just then a pick-up came by, with a couple of Indians. Seeing us looking distraught, they got out. 'What happened? Can we help?' they asked in English. I told them the story and we went in search of the thieves, who were now far out of sight.

'Oh no, our passports are in that bag,' I suddenly remembered. In Burundi, one had to be able to produce some form of identity at any time away from home or there would be trouble. Stella was due to fly to England for her second term at Roffey Place in just a few days. I walked under the large swaying leaves of the banana trees, thinking, 'A child does not worry how his father will answer his request. When he says, 'Daddy, I want this,' he expects it to appear. He doesn't wonder how many hours' work it will take to get enough money to buy it. He simply asks.' I looked up and said, 'Father, Daddy, I want my passport back.' Then I remembered the scripture in Mark 11:22–4 which says we must speak to the mountain and command it to be moved. We must not doubt but believe that what we say will happen and it will be done for us. I shouted out loud, 'Passport, come back here, in Jesus' name!' and I held out my hands.

We arrived home and told everyone what had happened.

'There's some chance you'll find it in the Post Office,' said David.

'What do you mean?' I asked.

'There is a special box where thieves return people's passports and no questions are asked. Your other things might be sold in the market,' he said, laughing.

We kept checking at the Post Office but nothing turned up. I held on in faith, squashing out the doubts.

'You're not still worrying about your passport, are you?' David said one day.

'No, I'm not worried,' I replied, at the same time breathing a prayer: 'Lord, You know what I've prayed. I'm still believing You.'

A friend of David's had contact with some of the thieves, as he had witnessed to many of them at the car-washing place beside the lake. Thieving in Bujumbura was a well-organised business. Different areas of town were sectioned off where groups would work under a leader accountable to the chief thief. David's friend managed to find the thieves who stole my bag, and came walking into the office triumphantly, passports in hand. Stella and I shouted and rejoiced in the Lord. He had done the impossible. A few days later we took Stella to the airport and waved her off, thanking God for His goodness.

I spent many hours driving David in the white Toyota minibus, meeting people and giving them lifts. I was happy to be a chauffeur, driving the left-hand-drive vehicle over roads I was unused to.

'OK, just stop here,' said David, preparing me for a tricky bit of driving.

'Oh, you can drive now,' I said, looking nervously at the stretch of mud and water along the road.

'No, you can do it,' said David confidently. 'Look for the best place to pass. Get the wheels in line and approach with speed. Then don't accelerate too much once you hit the mud.'

'Splash!' My fingers gripped the steering wheel and I gave a sigh of relief when we came out the other side of the large muddy puddle without slipping around too much. 'Thank You, Jesus,' I said out loud.

David was working hard and appreciated someone else driving him. He was helping over a thousand people who did not appear to be receiving the pastoral care they needed in their churches. I was certainly learning from his rather unique way of ministering. His genuine concern for people was so evident. He would often give away nearly all his money to pay people's hospital fees or feed a needy family or help someone in an emergency – and there were plenty of them. Day after day, David told incredible stories of the day's events. He was a man who heard God and was not afraid to step out in faith. Signs and wonders followed him daily.

In Bujumbura we held a conference. It was a very fruitful time. I liked the relaxed way David ministered using words of knowledge and praying for people to be healed. One young man had a dramatic encounter with the Lord. He exhorted the people, 'You must give your life to the Lord. These people are telling you the truth.'

Almost every week, I drove David up into the mountains to the Bible School in Nyakarago. The road was very winding with hardly a straight stretch and the view was spectacular. Green hills towered above us and the valleys dropped steeply down below. The cultivated mountains looked like patchwork blankets. On journeys like these, David often told me stories about his life.

At the sloping turn-off to the Bible School, the mud road was steep and the ruts gave me the impression that I could not drive the minibus down. But with some encouraging instruction from David, I succeeded. The third time I drove down that route I wondered what had worried me the first time.

The temperature change on the journey was unusual. It was like driving from a hot Spanish summer to a showery April in England within the space of forty minutes. We put on layers of clothes as we drove up and stripped off as we returned to the city. On my first drive down, David told me, 'Don't use the brakes too much.'

'Why not?'

'They may overheat and jam.'

So we came roaring round the bends using the gears to slow us down. What didn't help was that the back left-hand suspension had gone and the whole minibus veered over to one side where there was often a sheer drop below. Almost every week we came across overturned goods vehicles strewn across the road or abandoned in a valley. Needless to say, I prayed hard, but each journey became less stressful as I got used to the conditions.

The Bible College was set in a beautiful place. The buildings had been provided miraculously by God. I described the scene in a letter to Jan:

The sun is around somewhere although the sky is full of clouds. The air is deliciously clean, cool and crisp. I'm leaning up against a tree, sitting on my waterproof jacket. Straight ahead of me and running past on my right is a stream, gushing down in white, frothy torrents. There's a slight waterfall near me. The noise of the water is constant and calming. I can hear the cries of children and the pounding of bare feet over the surrounding hills as they make their way to the nearby school from all directions. There is the scraping, sizzling noise of tree insects. I'm surrounded by all kinds of trees: firs, eucalyptus (wonderful smell), avocado and many others which we don't see in England or Europe. It's very spongy with grass everywhere.

A massive pile of chopped logs lies a little to my left, ready for the evening fires and also for cooking. It's so beautiful in the evenings with the stillness, the glowing fire, the cold air and the rich sense of God's nearness. Beyond the logs is a group of buildings with lovely 'crazy paving' stone walls and tiled roofs. There's a tea plantation on the top of the hill beyond the eucalyptus trees. Behind are cultivated hills and groups of little round mud huts with thatched roofs. Shepherd boys carry sticks, leading small groups of cows and goats up and down the grassy slopes.

David taught at the Bible College. In the evenings we

sang and prayed around the open fireplace in one of the rooms, trying to keep warm. The atmosphere was cosy afterwards as we drank sweet tea without milk. Hushed voices murmured around the room. I could only communicate in English with James and Shadrack who had both been in Uganda. French was a necessity as I taught a whole class of students to speak English. It was amazing how fast they learnt.

'How did you become born again?' I asked Shadrack one day.

'Someone preached to me and I started reading the Bible for myself,' he told me. 'One of the first scriptures I read was, "Go into all the world and preach the gospel to every creature" (Mark 16:15 NKJ). So I had to do it, as I was now a Christian. I shared the little I knew about Jesus with my neighbours in the village. When I met someone who was ill I did what I had read in the Bible, and laid hands on them. Many people were healed and many turned to the Lord. So we had to start a church. The new converts spread the good news of Jesus Christ in the next village. Within a short time, five churches were planted in my area where there had been none before.'

'Did you hear God telling you specifically what to do or where to go?' I asked him.

'No,' he replied, 'I just read it in the Bible and obeyed.'

Many people wait for some profound revelation before they share Jesus. When God has already spoken, no sign is needed. We just need the power of the Holy Spirit to come upon us and be released out of us. It's not until we go and witness that we realise what God did when He filled us with the Holy Spirit. People are suffering, waiting for the Church to act.

One morning, I washed in the waterfall. It was freezing cold but very invigorating. Sometimes I walked for hours.

The sense of safety alone in that unknown country was amazing. People were always pleased to see me, and often intrigued to find out where I had come from. Occasionally I was followed by a crowd of children. How I longed to go into their houses and share the gospel, but most of these people were uneducated subsistence farmers so they had not learnt French. All I could do was smile and look to heaven and then point to them.

Once, a man invited me into a little mud hut. I greeted everyone in Kirundi and shook hands with an elderly gentleman who had six fingers on each hand. Inside the house, against one of the walls, was a kind of platform made of compacted mud with a reed mat placed on top. This was used as a bed. The floors and walls were smeared with cow dung which had dried. This prevented the house from becoming too dusty and the smell was not as bad as one might imagine. The kitchen was a tiny room where they cooked over an open fire. I felt privileged to have been welcomed into this family's home and wished I could have shared the experience with some of my English friends.

Many happy hours were spent talking to the Lord and exploring the magnificent surroundings. What a sense of freedom! The clock was no longer governing everything, yet many things could be achieved.

On one occasion, some of the Zaïrian students came down to the city from Nyakarago. Unfortunately they had no identity documents and were stopped by soldiers at the roadside, arrested and taken to prison. Thankfully, David soon heard of the incident and worked immediately for their release, visiting various officials. The following day he went to the prison with the relevant papers and a sense of dread, wondering what he would find. The conditions were harsh and beatings were not uncommon.

However, the students had not been mistreated. Instead they had used the opportunity to preach the gospel and many were convicted of their sins. Guards, officials and other prisoners had knelt in repentance in front of the Christians and the glory of God had filled the prison.

One day, I drove the minibus to Nyakarago full of mentally disturbed people from the healing centre. 'This could be interesting,' I thought to myself, jumping into the driver's seat. I guessed it might be a battle getting through the two regular road blocks. These people had no identity cards as they had recently been picked up off the streets and brought to Sororezo. If we happened to find a tough-hearted soldier, he could arrest the whole group and throw them in prison, and us too for transporting them.

As we approached the first stop-point where the soldiers always stood and checked each passenger, David said to me, 'Pray! We need a miracle.' I prayed silently, binding the evil spirits who would want to prevent these people from being set free by the power of Jesus. I asked for God's favour. We drove up to the soldiers, slowing down to a halt. Ten of them were huddled together on one side of the road and didn't even look up. One soldier walked over to us slowly. He had such a lovely smile. 'Is he an angel?' I wondered to myself. It was quite a change from a previous experience when I was convinced one soldier was trying to poke his rifle up my nose!

'Where are you going?' the man asked politely.

David told him and the man waved us on without asking for documents. As we drove out of earshot, David and I screamed our thanks to God at the top of our voices and laughed. The next road block was also no problem. They waved us on without stopping to check any of our documents. Jesus is Lord!

On a free day, I cycled to Ken's place along the dual carriageway singing, 'There is joy, joy, joy in the presence of the Lord.' I suddenly became aware of a red car careering towards me, totally out of control, with a panic-stricken man at the wheel. He had somehow jumped over the island between the carriageways and was heading straight for me, narrowly missing a taxi which was just turning. Time stood still and I tried desperately to move out of his path. Just in time he gained control, bits flying off his car. Phew! He missed me. He went speeding down the wrong side of the dual carriageway in what looked like a crazy fit. People in the nearby market made shocked noises and mutterings. I stood there amazed. It was as if Satan's destructive forces were aimed directly at me as I was praising God. God sent an angel and diverted the car just in time.

I cycled off, my legs wobbling. I didn't want to get infected by the fear all around, so I continued to praise Jesus. One man who had seen everything shouted, '*Vous avez de la chance!* You're lucky!' and I yelled back, '*Oui, c'est le Seigneur!* Yes, it's the Lord!' Praise the Lord, my Protector! I arrived safely at the Johnsons' for cookies and iced tea.

Sometimes as I drove along I felt like screaming to Jesus in carefree delight. At other times I had to battle against an onslaught of negative thoughts that crushed and brought despair. When I was full of praise, those destructive powers seemed so unreal, but at the time of attack it felt so true. I could sense the spiritual atmosphere over the country and I was learning not to be weighed down by any oppression. As a citizen of heaven, raised up and seated with Christ in heavenly places, it was not a case of fighting upwards through a cloud of heaviness in an attempt to reach God. He was already nearby and had promised He would never leave or forsake me.

In the early hours of one morning in October 1991, I was woken up by the sound of gunfire. It sounded very near, maybe two streets away from our house. I looked at the wooden head-rest and wondered what kind of protection it could give from a stray bullet. Then the scriptures I had memorised came to mind: 'The Lord is my strength and my shield. Of whom shall I be afraid?' I knew I was shielded by One much greater than anything around me. My thoughts went to King David's psalm: 'Though an army besiege me, my heart will not fear; though war break out against me, even then will I be confident.' An army was not besieging me, but with fighting all around, death was possible. I faced it head on. For me it would be no tragedy – but rather a victory and fulfilment of my final destiny. I had come to Africa ready to die and I knew the truth of Colossians 3:3: '[My] life is now hidden with Christ in God.' I was completely safe. God would not take me one second before my time. Thanking God that Jesus holds the keys to life and death, I drifted back to sleep.

In the morning, David and Ruth were concerned about me. 'Were you afraid?' they asked. We heard on the radio that civil war had broken out in the city and in various parts of the country. Everyone was confined to their houses and no one was allowed out into the streets. It was no coincidence that Ruth had bought more food than usual at the market. We did not hear much gunfire after that initial event, although news of killings was announced on the radio. A rumour was circulated that the rebels had poisoned the water supply. Thankfully we found this to be untrue. Towards the end of the week, we were all rather tired of staying indoors and decided it would be a good time to teach Ruth to swim in the next-door neighbour's pool. Ruth learnt quickly and soon ventured alone into the deep end.

'*Yesu ni wangu, wa uzima wa milele!* Jesus is mine, for life and for eternity!' sang David.

'Can you teach me that song?' I asked.

What fun it was swimming up and down, singing and laughing. The children were all lined up behind the reed fence straining to see us through the gaps. The pool was too deep for them to come and swim.

Suddenly we heard gunfire close by. 'What shall we do?' I asked David.

'There's no point getting out. We may as well die here,' he joked, lounging around in the water.

The next day, David was concerned about the staff up at Sororezo. 'They must have run out of food by now. Let's go and check on them,' he suggested. We loaded the minibus with some of our remaining food.

'It looks less suspicious if you drive,' he said.

'Why? Because I'm white?' I asked, adjusting to a new way of thinking.

'Yes,' he replied.

The streets were deserted as we entered the city. It looked like a ghost town. We were stopped seven times by groups of soldiers, but David explained that we were taking food for the workers and pointed to the back of the minibus. Each time, they let us go, until we finally reached the healing centre. Everyone was pleased to see us.

'How is it down in the city?' they asked.

'Our area isn't too badly hit,' we replied.

We unloaded the food. 'God is great!' they said, 'We've just finished our last bowl of *uji* [cornflour porridge] and that was all we had left.'

David and I returned home safely.

After only a week, it was announced on the radio that we were free to leave our houses, although for several days people were very reluctant to do so. This was not surprising in the light of recent events. One teacher at a mission school had stepped out of his house and was immediately shot in the leg. The soldiers were panicking, suspecting everyone to be rebels.

Gradually things returned to normal and the city came slowly back to life, although several hundred innocent people had lost their lives. One young man belonging to the International Fellowship told us of a bullet that came into his house, miraculously missing everyone. It was still imbedded in the wall to tell the tale.

This small war was nothing compared to the devastation of the fighting which started a year or so later and is still continuing as I write. It did not receive much coverage on international news, although every family has been affected and thousands of lives lost.

On Christmas Day I had a lovely time with the Whites. After Boxing Day the International Fellowship had a short trip to some hot springs four hours' drive from the city. Forty people came with their tents. We drove off the tarmac road along a track which eventually brought us to an open field with a couple of round, open-sided huts. We used these as a kitchen and a meeting place. The first night was an English-style wash-out: it rained so heavily that there were floods inside our tents. The next day was spent lounging in hot pools and then diving in a freezing cold waterfall pool a few metres away. On the last day, we baptised one of the men, a Russian doctor, in the river. We sat on the rocks and sang to the accompaniment of a guitar. In the evenings we sat round the log fire enjoying entertainment in the form of sketches, stories and songs.

As people packed up to go home, Sarah White walked

over to me. 'Would you like to stay a bit longer?' she asked.

'Can I?' I said, expectantly.

'Well, the boys want to stay but they need another adult to be here really.'

'Yes, that would be great,' I said automatically. 'Could you let David know what's happening when you get back?' I asked, confident that he wouldn't mind.

The seven of us survived on left-overs: eggy bread, bacon and corn-on-the-cob. In the afternoon we hiked up a steep mountain nearby. The view was breath-taking, and so was the exercise in that high altitude. Ken was leading, forgetting that Alex White was only eight years old. They went ahead, trying to cross a stream which was very rocky and slid down into the water holding hands and floundering about all over the place. It was one of those scenes which was funny to watch and dangerous at the same time. We turned back up the steep escarpment we'd just descended, and sat and ate nuts and popcorn which Ken's dad had brought back from the States. We continued happily on our journey, ready for a good soak in a bubbling hot spring at the bottom. In the evening, we sat round the log fire and listened to Joseph's testimony, which never seemed to come to an end.

'Why don't you summarise some of the stories?' I suggested after listening for an hour and a half, but he continued and we fell asleep by the glow of the ashes and later struggled to our beds.

'Let's stay another day,' one of the boys tried to persuade us.

'We can't,' said Ken, 'and anyway, we don't have enough food.'

We set off in Kennie's bright yellow van singing, 'We all live in a yellow minibus' and 'We'll be coming round the mountains when we come'. We were stopped at an identity checkpoint for an hour, when the soldiers insisted that we unload all the equipment and open our smelly washing. We drove a few miles further and stopped for a picnic. A man came up to us. 'You can't stop here,' he said, 'you're near a military base.' So we got back in and took a different route with fewer security checks, finally arriving safely back in Bujumbura.

3

Those who know their God

It's easy to see where people are going wrong,
but it takes skill and wisdom to bring the solution

'Here's your letter,' said David, handing me the envelope.
It was from my brother, Adrian (Adi), inviting me to
join his evangelistic music band, No Bad Thing, for two
weeks in Uganda. They had been asked to minister with
Robert Kayanja, the founder of many Miracle Centre
churches in that country. Robert had stayed with us in
England several times while in transit to America and
had seen the band in action. I was pleased this mission

coincided with my time in Burundi.

My passport was at Immigration for the renewal of my Burundi visa. David agreed to collect it and help me organise the trip. The flight was on Saturday, leaving at 6.00 a.m., and by Thursday I still did not have my passport as David had been taken up with several other commitments. He came home that evening with sad news: 'I'm sorry, but somehow Immigration has lost your passport.'

'Lost it? How can they lose it?' I exclaimed.

The other problem was that on Fridays the Immigration office was closed all day. 'Maybe God doesn't want you to go to Uganda,' David suggested.

'Or maybe the devil doesn't want me to go,' I replied. I had prayed at length about this trip and felt such an excitement. I sensed God would do something powerful and that my life would be changed.

The next day, David found some willing workers who went into the Immigration office on their day off. They spent the whole afternoon searching for my passport. At 5.00 p.m. David took me into Immigration to check on the progress.

'They've searched for five hours and they haven't found it. Come on, let's go,' said David, taking hold of my hand. In my spirit I said, 'No way! I'm not giving up; God wants me to go to Uganda.' David tugged on my arm and I dragged my feet unwillingly, praying silently. As we reached the door I heard a lady shouting in Kirundi. She came running to us with my passport in her hand. 'God, you're great!' I said joyfully.

Now all we needed was the person who was authorised to stamp the visa. As we were discussing what to do, David wandered out to the front of the building. To his amazement the woman we needed just happened to be jogging past the office. She came in and processed the visa while the others looked for the key to the cash box. Just then a man popped his head round the door to see why the office was open at such a time. He was the one with the keys!

'Great! That's done that. Now what?' I asked, as we jumped into the minibus and banged the doors. David drove speedily to the airline office, but it was after 5.00 p.m. and they had closed. Somehow the favour of God on David's life worked wonders in every situation. They let him in and he arranged for a ticket to be collected at the airport; payment could be made there in the morning. However, they needed dollars or pounds sterling, as I was a foreigner, and by now all the banks were shut. We had only Burundi francs. I considered that if God had brought me this far, He would certainly do the rest.

David dropped me off at home and went to the office, returning late in the evening. 'You'll never guess what. A friend of ours turned up at the office and happened to have dollars in her handbag. It's just enough to cover your ticket,' he said. The lady had not travelled out of the country. It was a mystery that she was carrying dollars. We marvelled at the way God works.

I didn't sleep much that night, partly because I had to wake up early to leave for the airport. By 5.30 a.m. I was washed, packed and eager to go, but the rest of the household were still not ready. In true African fashion they wanted to see me off at the airport, even though I'd only be away for two weeks.

'Come on, guys. We're late!' I shouted, somewhat anxiously. After God had worked so many miracles, I couldn't miss the plane now. I took my bag outside and got in the minibus and was soon followed by some of the others, still pulling their clothes on. Baby Sarah started to cry when she saw Mummy climbing into the vehicle.

'Come on. Let's go!' I insisted.

I tried to keep my heart calm, while David drove wildly, swerving to avoid potholes instead of braking. We reached the airport in time and checked my luggage through the X-ray machine. At the counter stood the clerk, proud of her uniform and her job. David spoke to her in French, explaining that my ticket should be there as promised.

'No! There's no ticket for her,' she said rudely. David and I stood in silence. I sensed the Lord's presence surrounding us as we sent up 'arrow' prayers.

'Could you check once more?' David suggested firmly but politely. She went out into the back room and returned with something in her hand. Amazed, she told us that although there was no ticket for me from the office in town, someone had cancelled their flight and for some reason the computer had not marked the name. She put the blank ticket down on the counter for David, who wrote in my name. We walked away gratefully.

We needed to pay for the ticket at another counter but it was locked and no one had arrived. Thankfully I was allowed into the departure lounge while David agreed to pay once the worker arrived. I skipped through triumphantly, waving happily at the little group of people who were seeing me off.

Sitting in the lounge I wondered if the people waiting for the same flight had struggled as much as I had to go to Uganda. We walked on to the runway and boarded a small, twenty-seater plane. The flight was amazing. We flew over Rwanda and I was fascinated at the little settlements dotted around, linked up by dirt roads running throughout the country. I was sitting two feet from the pilot in the front of the plane and could see his every move. The landing was great as we came down over Lake Victoria. At first I thought we might land in the water, but common sense told me to trust that the pilot knew what he was doing.

It just so happened that a friend of David's was on the same flight. The people who collected her took me to the Miracle Centre where Adi, his wife Justine and the rest of the group had arrived that morning from England. I had not managed to contact anyone in Uganda to let them know I was coming, so I was very grateful for the lift. As we drove up to the Miracle Centre, I spotted Justine and the gang leaving the church in a bus. I leapt out of the car and attracted their attention. Thanking the driver, I lifted my suitcase up into the bus. It was good to see everyone, having been away for nearly five months.

Within ten minutes we were at an open-air meeting in Makarere University. The band played and preached to about four thousand people, the biggest crowd they had ever ministered to.

We spent the first week ministering in meetings around Kampala. It was encouraging to be around Christians who pray. It felt like Roffey Place. I had walked into the middle of a move of God. Robert Kayanja had a house where many people were living and in the evenings some of us prayed on the roof. I got to know the Africans easily as there was no language barrier; English is Uganda's national language. By this time, my French had improved and almost become automatic so I kept saying '*merci*' and '*bonjour*'. The Ugandans just looked at me strangely.

I noticed that although the Ugandans still liked shaking hands, they did not spend quite so much time greeting one another as the Burundi people did. The Ugandans were more lively and energetic and the whole atmosphere of the country was different. Sometimes while praying on the roof I sensed a tremendous battle in the spirit realm. The gospel was moving ahead like wildfire but there was such resistance. Muslims could be heard wailing at various times of the night and once we were all woken by a goat screaming its lungs out because a thief was trying to untie it. People still spoke of the war during Idi Amin's time, and although they didn't give too many painful details, they did mention the suffering the country had known. Maybe that accounted for the lack of peace one felt. It was necessary to pray without ceasing, just to stay level-headed.

I had such admiration for Robert Kayanja. As a young man of twenty-nine, he had authority in God, yet remained humble. Everyone in the streets knew his name, both Christians and non-Christians. They heard about the miracles God performed through him. He had a regular slot on television and the crusade we were involved in was televised live each afternoon. Robert travelled internationally taking the message of the gospel and bringing revival to the hearts of Christians. Signs and wonders followed each time he preached. He was surrounded by many young evangelists, full of the Holy Spirit.

Chris, one of the team from England, was not a Christian when he came. He had been invited to help with the setting up of the equipment and to do the sound mixing. In one of the meetings when Robert ministered, the presence of God came into the meeting hall with such force, more like a hailstorm than like the dew. I heard a scream from behind and chairs scraping, people falling down, some laughing, some crying. God was at work, healing and delivering people. At the end of the meeting we found Chris leaning over the mixing desk, resting his head on his arms. The awesome presence of God had filled him with fear and he confessed his sins and acknowledged Jesus as Lord of his life. From that day, he was completely transformed. That's what you call being born again! Chris soon started preaching and enjoying hours of prayer.

In the second week, we travelled to a town called Jinja, where we camped down in an empty house. The girls were together in one room, two sharing a bed, and a Ugandan called Harriet and me on mattresses on the floor. I'll never forget the night I woke up with a cockroach on my nose. I sat up, spluttered about, and the two-inch-long creature scuttled off and rustled around in a polythene bag. I couldn't be bothered to get the torch so I just rebuked it in the name of Jesus and it stopped making a noise and left me alone for the rest of the night.

The crusade in Jinja was a great success. Since Reinhard Bonnke had been prevented from ministering there, no large mission had taken place. A wooden stage was set up and crowds streamed into the field. Rows of people sat on the roofs of distant houses and in the trees. Everyone sang and danced enthusiastically, even those who were not yet true Christians. The band played and different ones spoke in between songs. We soon became friends with the New Wave Band who ministered with Robert. After a couple of hours of music, Robert would come and share a word relevant to the people and then have an extended time of ministry to the sick and oppressed. In Jan's letter I wrote:

The crusade has been wild. Ten thousand people was the latest estimate, but the crowd expands each afternoon. What a way to change a town! Some walk from surrounding villages too. After a simple gospel message. Robert prays a prayer of authority and says, 'Promise me that when you're healed you'll come and tell everyone what Jesus has done.' Yesterday was amazing. Jesus was lifted up.

Cripples got off the floor to climb up a rickety

ladder on to the stage. A man totally blind for eight years saw. He touched Robert's nose, chasing him and copying him. He watched the crowd as we praised God with all our might. A five-year-old Muslim girl came with her sister. She had been deaf from birth and heard for the first time. 'Yesu!' (Jesus) she said into the mike. Three people who were wandering totally insane, some of them naked, came to the crusade ground. One man, who had been eating leaves in the bush, was instantly restored as Robert prayed a general prayer. He was amazed to find that he was naked. Someone gave him some clothes and the next day he shared his testimony on stage. Tumours disappeared, pain ceased, demons left. Oh Jesus! The joy! So many people were healed. The Holy Spirit was poured out. It's so natural. There's no hype or special atmosphere, but God is just there.

There was a Muslim girl who was blind in one eye. At the hospital, the doctor suggested that she come to the crusade. She was healed and gave her testimony on stage. Robert prayed with her for salvation in front of everyone. After the testimonies there is such rejoicing. The music starts and every-one dances and claps to Jesus. Robert is so excited at what God is doing.

What I could not get over was that these miracles happened every single afternoon, again and again. Blind eyes opened, deaf ears heard, cripples walked, tumours disappeared. These were like the days of Jesus and the early Church and I was seeing it happen all around me.

People visited us in the house where we were staying. I noticed a young pastor called Johnson Musegula who

Adi seemed to be particularly fond of. They went into the girls' room for some peace and quiet. I crept in to get something and found them praying. Johnson turned to me and prophesied. 'You're a great woman of God! Stop minimising yourself and concentrating on small, small things. God is going to use you mightily.' That was an encouraging surprise. I knew God was speaking.

The evangelistic fire which had been in me years ago was once again being stirred up. Life in Burundi had been good. It was a non-pressure place where I could get accustomed to African ways. It seemed like a sabbatical after the intense work at Kingdom Faith, and I knew the coming season would be more stretching. It often bothered me to see bad situations when Christians reacted in the flesh instead of behaving as Spirit-filled born-again people. I would go away and pray seriously and find scriptures speaking directly into the circumstances, but somehow I never had the courage to speak out. So things remained the same and I was frustrated. But I knew God was asking me for more. 'How can you be so selfish and keep all that good teaching to yourself?' If they heard the Word some of the difficulties in relationships would never occur. But it was easier for me to hide than to be in the forefront.

Of course, God had His way. One evening in Jinja I went into the garden to pray. I paced up and down, thanking God for everything He was doing. I started preaching to the Lord and stopped myself after a couple of minutes. 'Hang on a minute. God knows this stuff. Why am I telling Him?' I asked. Then the answer came: 'This is the message you'll be preaching tomorrow.' It was a fleeting thought which I could have easily brushed aside, but I paid attention just in case it was God speaking. I really didn't want to preach, but I told the Lord, 'If this is You, I'll do it. But You'll have to arrange it for me.'

As I slept that night, the message was buzzing around in my mind. 'Once you were alienated from God and were enemies in your minds because of your evil behaviour. But now he has reconciled you by Christ's physical body through death to present you holy in his sight, without blemish and free from accusation – if you continue in your faith, established and firm, not moved from the hope held out in the gospel' (Col. 1:21–3). In the morning I walked down the corridor outside the boys' room, where one of the pastors was talking to my brother. I overheard him saying, 'Can you preach in my church this morning?'

'We've got a music practice and we need to prepare for the crusade. Sorry,' Adi said, looking up as I walked by. 'Maybe my sister could preach though,' he added. 'Hey Anth, would you like to preach in their church this morning?'

'Yes, OK,' I replied, amazed at my own answer. Had the Lord not spoken to me the night before I would never have taken up the offer.

'We'll come and collect you at 11.00,' the pastor told me.

I rushed back to my room and started praying fervently before fear could set in. I knew from my time with Colin that the battle could not be won from the pulpit, but only in the prayer room. So I prayed wholeheartedly. Faith won the battle and I went joyfully to the church. People were singing and I was grateful for more time to pray. As I stilled myself before Him, the Holy Spirit gave me some words of knowledge for people who needed healing.

'OK. I'll do that after the preaching,' I thought.

'No, you'll do it first,' the thought came back. 'This is my meeting.'

'Yes, Lord,' I replied.

So they introduced me and I started to speak. '*Imana shimwe!* Praise God!' Everyone looked at me, including my mystified interpreter. 'Oh no, sorry, that's Kirundi – wrong language. *Mukama yebazibwe!* Praise God! [in Luganda]'

'*Amina!* Amen!' they shouted in reply.

'It's good to be with you today,' I began. 'As I was sitting here I felt the Lord wanted to heal someone with a problem in the left knee and someone else with jaw ache. Are those people here?'

The woman with the knee problem came forward. She stood in the front and raised her hands up to heaven. These people were ready for the visitation of God. Several people with jaw ache also came forward. All of them were healed immediately by the power of God as I laid hands on them. Everyone saw what happened and people's hearts were ready for the message. Instead of looking at me, a young, slim, white girl, they realised that God was with me and that He had something to say.

After preaching, I prophesied and prayed for an hour over individuals. One man who found walking very painful was healed in a second; a partially blind girl was also healed and those who were demonically oppressed were set free. Jesus was glorified and I walked back to the house satisfied. The preaching had really flowed, even with an interpreter who was not used to my accent. Now the devil could never convince me that I couldn't preach. The ice had been broken and I was launched. On this trip, God had deposited something lasting in me.

The flight home over the mountains was very turbulent. I nearly lost my breakfast, but we started the descent just in time. It was lovely to be picked up by someone at the airport and driven home. The peace in that country descended on me again. Uganda and Burundi were so close and yet so different. Everything in Burundi was so much more laid back.

Don Double and the Good News Crusade came to Burundi to evangelise the town of Gitega. As far as we knew, it was the first crusade ever to take place there. His organiser, Pete, arrived early and we travelled together and had a great time talking about what the Lord had done in our lives. There was so much joy inside and laughter outside.

We stayed in a guest house in Gitega for a few days while making arrangements for the crusade. At the breakfast table David told me, 'I had so many dreams last night. In one of them, I dreamt that the president of Burundi came to visit our clinic at Sororezo.' He spoke quietly, as if almost afraid to mention it. However, within a week the dream had been fulfilled. The president landed on the mountain in his helicopter and we were all on Burundi television as he was shown around the clinic.

The crusade was great. The Lord worked miracles and many responded to the message of salvation. The meeting had a different flavour to the ones in Uganda, the people and the ministers being different. It was a privilege to be part of the crusade.

One week later, having said goodbye to my friends in Burundi, I returned to England. What a blessed time it had been. I learnt such a lot from David and I was looking forward to whatever God had for me next.

While writing this chapter, I received the shocking news that David was killed in a plane accident in Zaïre, together with thirteen pastors and six aid workers. He was on his way back from a wonderful crusade where many thousands of people turned to the Lord. There were no survivors from the accident and the burial took place at the site. Over thirty-two thousand attended. Praise God for the life of David which influenced many in Burundi, Rwanda and Zaïre as well as in other parts of the world. He was a greatly loved man and many people will miss him.

4

Take up your Cross

The general public don't care if I live or die;
why worry about what they think?

In England it was not easy to adjust to a completely
different life. People seemed to talk so fast and the speed
of the advertisements on television made me dizzy. I had
changed so much, but everything at home was going on
the same as usual. Burundi seemed like another world to
me. I stayed with my brother and his wife and stuck a big
map of Africa on the wall, which I often looked at while
lying on my bed. Kingdom Faith were having three weeks

of revival meetings to launch the church. God was on the move. I felt very much at one with the vision, but somehow I knew I was not supposed to fit back into the scene at KF. Africa had become my home.

During my short stay in Uganda, two members of Miracle Centre had invited me to return and hold crusades with them. They often organised evangelism in the villages and had even planted some small churches. This was just the kind of experience I needed but my heart sank when I thought of preaching to crowds of people. I had to conquer that fear.

There was no point sitting back waiting for the ideal opportunity. It might never come. Here was an open door and I simply needed to book my ticket and go. So I cornered myself into the position where it would be impossible to avoid preaching. I could learn as I went along. Robert Kayanja came to Horsham to minister in my old church. He was excited to hear that I wanted to visit Uganda. He invited me to stay in his house.

I had been inspired watching God at work through the Ugandans and wanted to find out what it cost them for Him to move in such a way. I was not content to have had an amazing trip to Uganda and to be able to speak about the miracles I had seen. I wanted the Kingdom of God to be manifested through my lifestyle, rather than speaking about God's wonders as if they were history. It was all very well to go back full of fire because of what I'd seen, but I wanted those things to become a normal part of my life. That would mean paying a price; I would have to change. If I slumped back into the comfortable status quo I would be more popular and less challenging to others, but I would not be in the will of God. Being a nice Christian, full of smiles, was fine, but where was the fruit? It was good to sing the songs, but what about the action?

Jesus said, 'Anyone who has faith in me will do what I have been doing. He will do even greater things than these, because I am going to the Father' (John 14:12). I needed to experience this on a greater level.

I raised money for my ticket, but had no spending money until my stack-stereo was stolen; I received a cheque from the insurance company two days before leaving for Uganda. At Entebbe Airport I looked in vain for a familiar face.

'Taxi? Taxi? Taxi?' The words bombarded my unruffled nerves. I tried to phone Kampala but could not get through. Eventually I took a taxi, haggled unsuccessfully and was over-charged, as I couldn't remember the exchange rate.

At Robert's house, Harriet ran to welcome me, surprised that I had actually come. Robert was still out of the country on ministry. 'He's coming back any time,' I was told, so I put my disappointment aside. The house was like a rabbit warren with every available space occupied; there were fifteen Ugandans and two European visitors who had come to preach. Pastor Godfrey let me sleep in his room in the basement for my first night, as he was away. The following night I slept on the roof of the house under the stars, which was fun until it rained. The alternative was the floor of a stuffy garage with Harriet and two young girls. In the morning one of the visitors saw me emerging with bags under my eyes.

'Where are you sleeping?' he asked, sounding concerned.

'In the garage, on the roof.'

'Oh no, use my room and I'll move in with the other visitor,' he insisted.

My earplugs were a life-saver as the television blasted full volume through the thin walls until 2.00 a.m. most nights, and at 5.00 a.m. the whole household would be woken by someone praying loudly. I was not used to this kind of life, but I was grateful to have a bed and a mattress. Most of the young lads were on mats on the floor; some of them were orphans whose parents had died in the war.

It was good to have Godfrey around. He was full of fun and could understand my English accent as he had spent several months abroad. I helped him and Fiona with their last-minute wedding preparations. They had a slight set-back two days before the wedding when Fiona's handbag was stolen. It contained £100 cash, Fiona's wedding ring and two watches. The bag disappeared from beside her bed as she slept. It looked as if someone had managed to reach it through the open window, using something to catch the handle. They thought they knew who the thief was and their suspicions were confirmed when they saw one footmark in the dusty ground outside the room where Fiona had been sleeping. It was someone with one leg who had hooked the bag up with one of his crutches. The missing bag was never found but people were generous and money was quickly raised to replace what was lost.

The wedding was amazing. Somewhere between three and four thousand people turned up at the Miracle Centre and afterwards seven hundred went to the reception on the other side of town where an indoor stadium had been hired. I was given the honour of serving on high table. Among all the black faces I looked eagerly to see if I could recognise anyone. Yes! There was Pastor Johnson. He shook my hand with such respect that tears came to my eyes. The last few days had been hard. People were reacting strangely towards me and I didn't understand why. If I knew the thinking behind their behaviour I could adapt myself to the country and the people's ways. But there was no one to answer my questions. I just hoped that people would quickly get to know and understand me.

A rumour circulated that I had come to marry a member of the music group. A young girl took me aside, telling me to reconsider it as many girls in the church wanted to marry him and they would put a curse on me. I couldn't believe my ears. The thought of marriage was far from my mind. I had come to learn how to preach. I wanted God to use me. Why couldn't people understand? I told the girl, 'I've come here to preach the gospel and that's my only motive. And anyway, God has blessed me, so how can I be cursed?'

'You may say that, but it takes very great faith not to be affected,' she continued.

'Yes, my faith in God is very strong. He is my strength,' I replied firmly. 'Gossip is very disruptive to the work of God, you know. I wouldn't get involved in it if I were you.' I walked away, shocked at the thought of so-called Christians cursing others.

That first week was a terrible time. There was such a fierce attack on my thoughts and emotions. I felt like a shirt that had been through a spin-drier. Now Jesus was walking about inside me, and the real challenge was to hold on to my identity in Christ. Surrounded by so many negatives, I had to keep affirming the truth. I missed the safety of the loving, caring environment of Roffey Place where people were becoming united in the faith. Few people in the house understood English. With those who did, I had to speak clearly and slowly, repeating everything many times. I felt left out, especially when everyone was enjoying a joke. I would listen to the unfamiliar sounds of the Luganda language, desperate to learn it.

Living with us was a nineteen-year-old evangelist. He arrived back from hospital, having been ill with meningitis. 'God moved mightily!' he told us. 'The nurses challenged me, "If you're really a man of God, why don't you do something?" I was so sick, people thought I would die. A little girl on the bed next to me died and although I was attached to a drip I prayed for her, breathed on her and God brought her back to life. The doctors and nurses were amazed. I told them it was the power of Jesus Christ, the Son of God. Another man was healed of asthma and gave his life to the Lord.' These types of miracles were common in the life of this evangelist, on street corners, in shops, in the taxis, in the market. The life of Jesus was flowing through.

I soon started preaching, but it was a struggle. I didn't feel myself at all. Not only was I learning to preach but I was dealing with a different culture. Under David's covering in Burundi, I had not had to adapt too much. Here in Uganda I felt as if I was putting on an act, trying to behave as people expected me to, so I could fit in with society and avoid too many confrontations and strange reactions. I ministered at a ladies' meeting and then at a church outside Kampala, where I preached to a crowd of four hundred people from the balcony of a house and prayed for the sick. One elderly man wanted prayer for his neck. No one had to tell me what he did for a living. He smelt of cows from head to toe.

The following week we held a crusade in a war-torn village one hour's drive from Kampala. We were invited by a man who was running an orphanage there. We faced all kinds of problems setting it up. Harriet and I had our photos taken and a poster designed to advertise the crusade. We went to the printers and paid an extortionate amount of money to produce copies. They promised to finish the work in time, but each day we checked and they told us, 'Come back tomorrow.' When the crusade had already ended, they were finally ready. There were other frustrations too. Some Christians tried to sabotage the crusade, for no reason I could understand. However, we pressed on, and I couldn't help thinking how different this was from the well-organised, orderly ministry I had previously been accustomed to.

For the first crusade meeting, we set off three and a half hours late.

'Is it really worth going now?' I asked.

'Yes, the people will be expecting us,' the Ugandans insisted.

When we arrived, the crowds gathered around me as if I was an animal in the zoo – they were not used to seeing white people in that area. We set up the PA equipment in the grassy field. Someone went to speak to the man who had agreed to let us use electricity from his house, and came back looking rather gloomy. 'The man's changed his mind.' We were stuck. There was no other building nearby and we had no generator. A group from our team discussed with the man. Twenty minutes later he agreed to let us use it, but at an unreasonable price, maybe because he saw that white people were involved. Somehow he was persuaded to lower the price and we began.

Someone prayed a powerful prayer, three ladies led the singing and then I stood up with my interpreter to preach. 'How many people here are already saved?' I asked. Only ten people put up their hands. Now I knew who I was speaking to. I kept the message short and was followed by another preacher. By the end of the evening, thirty adults and fifty children had responded to the challenge of following Christ. We called the sick to come forward and Harriet prayed. 'Now do what you couldn't do before,' she instructed. People started to stretch and bend and those who had been healed came to the front. A mother brought her little girl forward.

'What was wrong with your daughter?' Harriet asked.

'She couldn't hear well,' she told the crowd, holding the mike nervously.

'How long was she like that?' asked Harriet.

'Since she was very small, she's never been able to hear or speak properly,' the lady replied.

'Now what has happened?'

'God healed her!' shouted the mother, waving her arms in the air.

A roar went up from the crowd as they tested the little girl's hearing.

'That was a good start,' we agreed as we drove back with the equipment. With all the problems, the crusade had nearly been cancelled.

'If it hadn't been for you standing with me, I would have given up. But now you see what God has done,' Harriet said.

'God is great!' I exclaimed, thinking of all the people whose lives had been changed.

I woke up early in the morning and prayed for rain. It was so hot. There was no running water in the house due to low water pressure in the area. A young lad with a bike occasionally brought lake water in jerricans for us to buy. We boiled it before drinking – it didn't taste too bad but the bits of weed floating about were rather off-putting. And washing in a bowl of water two inches deep was not great in that climate.

When the first drops of rain fell, I rushed to put on my swimming costume, grabbed my shampoo and ran outside to stand under the water shooting off the roof through a pipe. The Ugandans tried to hide their amusement at my squeals, as torrents of cold water poured over me. The force of the water hurt my head, but I didn't mind. I felt gloriously clean.

That day we arrived too late to collect the vehicle to take us to the crusade. But kind Sister Ruth offered us a lift in her car. I waited at Ruth's shop for Harriet for over an hour and finally she turned up. Harriet was the sort of person who, if I said I was leaving right now, would quickly grab her clothes and rush to the bathroom to wash, emerging an hour later, dressed in neatly ironed clothes, skin shining and every hair in place. I hasten to add that she has improved in that area considerably since then.

Incidentally, it was interesting to see how important dress is to the Ugandans. They could sacrifice food for a week, to pay for one good outfit. Some people dressed as if for a wedding just to go into town. I remember a strange reaction from some of the pastors when they found me at home washing my clothes by hand and wearing shorts. It wasn't until months later that I realised it was shameful for a woman to show her knees or thighs. Even for a woman to wear trousers was not acceptable, and in past regimes she could have been shot dead on the spot for such an offence. No one had explained such things to me, and I was left wondering why people reacted the way they did.

Ruth's car broke down and we arrived late for the crusade, so the next day we used public transport. Kampala taxi park is a remarkable sight, with about a hundred minibuses squeezed together into one area. At first glance it appears to be utter chaos, but actually there is order and very few drivers bump as they find their way to the exit. The minibuses are designated certain areas according to where they are going. Young conductors shout their taxi's destination. It's pandemonium with everyone calling out at the same time:

'Luwero, Luwero, Luwero!'
'Rubaga, Rubaga!'

'Mbale, Mbale, Mbale!'

It sounds like a market-place, only noisier and rougher. People board a taxi and sit until every seat is taken. Then the driver jumps in and off they go, fleeing the taxi park like wasps escaping from the neck of a bottle. They stop at intervals along the way to let passengers disembark or to collect people waiting at the roadside. Sometimes taxi drivers race, competing for passengers, which makes their driving hazardous, to say the least.

In the taxi park, purple-grey clouds emerged and the rain poured down, drenching everyone as they ran in a mad panic to get out of the deluge. We found our taxi; after travelling for an hour, I was startled by a noise coming from under the seat in front of me. A woman had brought two chickens with her, which suddenly squawked and clucked. I roared with laughter but no one else thought it was funny.

Once again the crusade was worthwhile. A young man I had spoken to earlier stood before the crowd. 'For two years I suffered with severe pains in the stomach. As many of you know, I was forced to give up my studies. I came to this crusade although I was a Muslim,' he said, watching the faces of his seven Muslim brothers, 'and when we prayed to God, I was healed. Mohammed never healed me, but Jesus healed me and now my life belongs to Him.' Any bad reaction in the crowd was covered up by people jumping, screaming and waving their hands in the air. The name of Jesus had been lifted up.

The next day, arrangements for the crusade were still not good. I was fed up. God created the world out of chaos, but surely the ministry didn't have to run like this. What made it worse was my physical state. I had not slept properly for a single night so far in Uganda and always woke up covered with mosquito and flea bites. There was no privacy. People walked through my room to use the bathroom, and meals arrived at such haphazard times, if at all. I stayed behind to pray that evening. I was so tired of the pressure. People looked to me as if I was a never-ending source of financial supply, and I had already used half of the money which was supposed to last me for three months.

When the others had gone, I went on to the roof in the evening sunlight. The high-rise buildings of Kampala were in view on the left and there were hills with houses and lots of greenery straight ahead. Lake Victoria could be seen to the right. I looked around the garden. The grass looked lush and green and there were various palm trees, a mango tree and brightly coloured flowers in the beds.

I began to pour out my heart to the Lord. 'I want to get out of here. Can I book myself on the next plane home? This is not what I expected.'

The Lord replied as clear as anything: 'You know who'll have the victory if you go now, don't you?'

I sat in silence, weighing up the statement in my mind. 'There's no way he's having the victory,' I declared. 'I'm staying, come what may.' I walked down the steps of the roof, satisfied that no matter what the circumstances, God was working out His purposes. This was a time of death to self, death to my desires and my physical comfort. I felt confident that the resurrection power of Jesus would be evident in and through my life.

The next day, Harriet and I both woke up with the same scripture for the crusade: 'If my people, who are called by my name, will humble themselves and pray and seek my face and turn from their wicked ways, then I will hear from heaven and forgive their sin and will heal their land' (2 Chron. 7:14). We were united in our mission. We sat around waiting for the pick-up to arrive. When it finally came we were told, 'There's no money for petrol.' I didn't have any Ugandan shillings with me and the only way I could get money would be to change my traveller's cheques in town. But I had no witness from the precious Holy Spirit that I should do this yet again.

As we sat in the lounge, all eyes were on me. I told them I had no money but they found it hard to believe. The pressure intensified and after forty minutes I explained again: 'Listen, I don't have the money here in the house and even if I did, I don't think I should pay for the transport this time. The Holy Spirit is restraining me.'

I walked out of the room and a few moments later, Harriet ran to me. 'Let's go!' she called.

'I thought you said we didn't have any money for petrol,' I quizzed.

'No, we have the money now.'

'Where did that suddenly appear from?' I asked, but there was no reply. I later discovered that someone had been given money for the crusade and was hoping I would pay for petrol so he could keep it. Praise God for the Holy Spirit's instruction. I'm no fool when I'm close to Him.

I sat in the back of the pick-up, my shoulders burning in the sun. I was wearing a double-layered skirt and I wrapped the outer layer over my arms and shoulders. We drove into a cloudy area and it poured with rain. The two of us in the back of the pick-up crouched close to the driver's cabin so that most of the rain went over our heads while we continued at a good speed. I was fine perched on the spare tyre, but my fellow passenger was sitting in a rapidly growing puddle. The rain started coming down in sheets and the driver slowed right down. 'Don't stop! Keep going!' we shouted, but he couldn't hear us above the sound of the rain on the tin roof. He pulled over and stopped. Within a second we were drenched as the momentum of the wind no longer carried the raindrops over our heads. Soon the sun came out and we went on our way again. I stood up to blow-dry my skirt and my hair. Suddenly I realised that although my clothes were getting dry, the back of my very full skirt was flapping up in the wind, leaving nothing to the imagination of the people by the roadside. Needless to say, I sat down rather abruptly, and chuckled out loud for several minutes.

We jumped out of the vehicle at the crusade ground and I went straight away to preach, still wet and be-draggled. I soon forgot about myself and preached a short message of hope. Once again people were saved and healed. There were two amazing testimonies from the day before. One lady had gone almost blind and Jesus restored her sight, and a deaf lady heard! Hallelujah! The gospel was starting to have an impact on that whole area as people heard of the miracles God had done. This was a close-knit community and they knew each other well, so the whole village was affected.

One man came up to Harriet, asking, 'Are you going to leave us now and stay in Kampala? We've left our life of sin and we don't want to go back to it. We need help.'

I spoke to the man who had invited us for the crusade. There were seventy new babes in Christ who needed spiritual nurturing. He agreed to begin a church in the orphanage and promised to pastor them, so that our work would not be wasted. I was relieved to hear that. What a privilege it was to be used by the Lord to save people from hell. If we had not gone there, those people's lives would not have been changed by the power of God.

Our next mission was to a village outside Jinja. It was good to be going back to that peaceful town again. The Rubaga Miracle Centre pastors in Kampala had organised a crusade and teaching seminars, and they had great expectations. I was asked to squeeze in the back of a pick-up, together with the PA equipment, the musical instruments and other people and children. By the end of the journey, my legs were completely dead and I was frozen through because we travelled after dark and the wind whipped us as we went. 'Oh well, mark this one down, Lord. Here I am, suffering for the sake of the gospel,' I prayed.

Our first night was spent in a mosquito-infested, cockroach-ridden place. I slept on the floor of a cell-like room adjoining a large room where some European visitors and an African prince were staying. I was woken out of a deep sleep by the sound of raucous laughter and one of the men saying, 'I heard it drop on your bed.' Looking through the crack in my door, I could see one of the men, in his underpants, flapping about in a panic, shoe in hand. Lizards and cockroaches were landing all over the place. Finally the men settled down, switched the torch off, and all was quiet, until – thud! The Scottish guy had thrown his shoe on the Norwegian's bed and the laughter started all over again, lasting for about an hour. What a crazy night.

Our second night was also eventful. We were taken to the house of a family where there were ten children. The mother looked so young I hardly dared believe that she had given birth to all of them. I slept in a stuffy room full of beds, the husband of the house in the bed next to mine, the wife and the two youngest children on the floor. Various people came in and out of the room all night through the squeaky door which was near my head. They knew no English and kept staring at me.

I went out in the night to find the toilet, a small wooden hut with a hole in the ground and a great drop below. To get there, one had to walk a plank over a quagmire where some ducks were paddling. I wondered how on earth I would manage to stay there for a whole week, especially as they started cooking at around 10.00 p.m. and usually ate at midnight. By that time the heat of the day and lack of lunch had sapped my energy so I was already asleep. At least I was used to fasting. The living conditions didn't seem so bad after a while, but I certainly had no excess flesh on my body by the end of the week. One evening, I was given a steaming dish of pork and rice. I noticed a fly in the first spoonful and delicately removed it, only to discover that the whole plate was swimming with flies, which I chose to ignore in my hungry state, having not eaten a decent meal for days.

The crusade meeting began well with Godfrey preaching from Isaiah 53: 'Who has believed our message and to whom has the arm of the Lord been revealed?' It was powerful preaching and his praying showed such intimacy with his Heavenly Father. The crowds numbered about four thousand, and people responded wholeheartedly. During the week about five hundred were saved, and many hundreds healed. I was told that usually three-quarters of those who respond are genuinely born again and commit themselves to the Church.

One very precious thing happened. A drunkard came into the crusade ground, totally out of himself. When he heard the gospel, he came forward crying and knelt in front of the stage, holding his head in his hands. The preacher stopped and prayed with him and he settled down for the rest of the meeting. The man was given some clothes to replace the rags draped over his body, and the following day he came back, looking completely different. He stood on the stage and spoke to the people: 'After the crusade meeting, my uncle offered me some alcohol to drink, but as soon as I put the cup to my lips, I vomited.

The power of Jesus has saved me and I will never drink again.'

The church building was a 'shack' made of bamboo woven together to form walls, and the people sat on wooden benches for hours. It was cool inside and a breeze came through the gaps in the wall. Sitting there in the front of the church, I had a shock.

'Now we have someone here with us today all the way from England,' began one of the pastors. 'Let's put our hands together as we welcome this great Bible teacher.' Everyone clapped and waited for me to stand up. I had not been asked to teach and I was certainly not prepared. I felt totally inadequate surrounded by those who were much more experienced than me. The Ugandans insisted that I say something, so I launched out and thankfully the words started flowing. After a while I stopped, as there were so many preachers waiting for their sessions, but the pastor motioned with his hand. 'Keep going. There's more,' he said. But I meekly took my place. Not being a talkative person by nature, I had no more words to fill in. I wanted only to speak the Word of God, but I was still learning how to let it flow.

I had more confidence while worshipping. I could come into the Lord's presence and sing in front of a crowd of people without any nervousness, but preaching was a different matter. 'Teach me how to do it,' was my constant prayer. Sometimes it was frustrating because I would say something funny and no one would laugh, or other times people would start laughing when it was not meant to be funny at all. Maybe the interpreter added humorous comments or perhaps it was just the culture difference. If I quoted too many scriptures, their minds wandered off. The concentration span of the less educated was short and one had to be enthusiastic and jump around and use illustrations to keep their attention, otherwise they would doze off and miss even the best teaching.

Many Christians here did not value teaching as much as we do in the West. They loved seeing the miracles, signs and wonders, but when it came to the character of Christ being developed in a person, or living a holy life, the interest faded. I knew I had something to give these people. I felt so rich and full, but how to give it was another matter. One day I said to the Lord, 'OK. If shouting makes them believe this is You, then I'll shout.' I didn't want to fall into the trap of imitating another preacher, but the message had to get across. So I experimented with different ways of ministering, trying to develop something new while still being myself.

One afternoon, we drove to a beautiful place along Lake Victoria. It looked like the Sea of Galilee. It was a clear day and the colours were crisp and bright. A shepherd made his way past our group with a herd of cows, their horns pointing up to heaven. This was a lovely setting for baptism. Fifty converts from the crusade were immersed in water. We prayed for them to receive the Holy Spirit and laid hands on them at the lakeside. I went off discreetly to enjoy a swim afterwards. What a relief it was to cool down the body temperature.

When the mission was over, I came back to Kampala, but it wasn't long before I was off again to a town called Busia on the border between Uganda and Kenya. There was a good Miracle Centre there and the pastor was a lady my age. God was using her to heal many sick people and she was called out to people's houses, almost like a doctor, where she first preached to the household and then laid hands on the sick. People travelled long distances to receive their miracles.

Miriam, a member of the New Wave Band,

accompanied me to Busia. We got on well, especially as her English was fluent. She was my interpreter and also preached. The turn-up at the church was not the best due to the rain and the fact that there were only a few iron sheets on the roof at that stage, but the people were easy to relate to and ready to listen. I taught about the Holy Spirit. We had a practical session where we split into groups and people prayed for each other using the gifts of the Holy Spirit. A couple of years later, I heard that God had used some specific words of knowledge and pro-phecies to launch people's ministries into existence. One was for a young man who I said had a pastor's heart. He was praying about pastoring a small church in a village and was grateful for the confirmation.

Out of all the prophetic words that were given, the one that no one believed was when I called a girl to the front and prophesied she would marry a pastor. She was dirty and uneducated. When I returned to that town two years later, she was a changed person. She had been living in Nairobi and was due to marry one of the pastors in Busia the following Saturday.

The ministry was enjoyable. The people were with me, lapping up the teaching. Their open faces were delightful and I sensed God's work in their lives would remain. I prayed for several who were sick and as I laid hands on them, a thought came to me: 'These people are not going to be healed. If someone else prayed for them they would be, but not if you pray.' I recognised it as a fiery dart from the devil and dismissed it, continuing to pray for the people. In the last five minutes, people stood up to glorify God with healing testimonies. It was a great encourage-ment.

An offering was taken. People danced to the front with their gifts. As well as money, they brought other items such as blankets, plates and even a duck with its legs tied together, and placed them on a mat on the mud floor. We gathered round to give thanks to the Lord. I kept my eyes open and saw the duck waddling out of the church. 'The offering is trying to escape,' I whispered to Miriam, and she got the giggles.

We had good fun together sharing a room and sleeping on two mattresses on the floor. One evening I spotted a rat running across the beam above our heads and I heard its dropping falling on my pillow in the night – all part of what it means to minister in Africa!

5

Fruit that will Last

Be bold towards God;
Be strong towards the devil;
Be confident with people.

My friend Liz was due to visit me for two weeks. She had written to me a month earlier, mentioning the date she hoped to come. The day before, I had still received no confirming letter but when I prayed, I sensed she would be arriving.

I woke up early in the morning; Harriet was already up and dressed and the breakfast table had been laid. We left

72

the house at around 6.00 a.m., using three taxis to get to the airport: one taking us into town, another taking us to Entebbe town and yet another dropping us off at the airport. We arrived in time and waited with all the other people at the glass windows overlooking the runway. The plane landed, and a very tired-looking Liz came down the steps and walked across the tarmac. 'That's Liz!' I told Harriet enthusiastically. When she was within earshot, I shouted out of the window, 'Lizzie! Lizzie!' She looked up, smiled and waved.

Harriet and I went downstairs and waited for Liz to go through Immigration and collect her luggage. We watched as each trolley pushed against the swing doors, with Indians, Chinese and Africans coming through.

'There's a white pair of hands,' I said, almost to myself. Yes, it was Liz. We hugged and Harriet pushed her trolley outside.

'Did you get my letter?' Liz began.

'I got one about three weeks ago,' I answered.

'Wow. How did you know I was coming, then?' she asked.

'I just sensed you would. It must have been the Holy Spirit,' I replied.

'So you don't even know what's been happening to me,' she said, shaking her head. 'It's a miracle I'm here. I've been flat on my back for the last two weeks with back pain, unable to move. I prayed with your mum and someone at church had a word of knowledge that it was God's will that I come. I crawled to the phone to book my flight, and I'm believing God that I'll be healed.'

Of course the Lord honoured her faith and it didn't take long before the pain left her back and we were able to do all kinds of things she had not imagined possible. Johnson Musegula had promised to arrange some ministry for us. He lived in the town of Jinja where he and a group of young men had pioneered a couple of Miracle Centre churches during an incredible move of God in the 1980s. In Jinja, Liz and I met up with some Americans from Oral Roberts University who had come to work with Miracle Centre in evangelism. We decided to combine forces and went together into schools and colleges preaching the gospel. We had a good time, especially in the nurses' school, as Liz herself was a trainee nurse.

After we had all spoken in a girls' boarding school, Johnson had a vision and asked the girls, 'Has anyone been oppressed by bad dreams and other evil attacks?' More than fifty girls responded, and as he prayed the power of God came down. Some screamed, some cried and others fell over and were set free. 'Those dreams will never come back again, in Jesus' name. The attack on this school is finished!' said Johnson, using his God-given authority. It was a breakthrough for that school.

After a week of schools work, Liz, Johnson and I travelled to a town called Iganga and met up with two pastors who were taking us to a newly planted church in the bush. Four months before, Pastor Edward had been ministering in Jinja and heard terrible news from his home village. Neighbours who used to be friends were breaking into each other's houses and stealing things. There were even some murders. He went with a group of Christians and preached to them in order to break that spirit which was trying to destroy the people. Their evangelism was a success and a group of fifteen people seriously repented of their sins and chose to follow Jesus.

As there was no effective church in that place, they started meeting under a tree outside the family home of Pastor Edward. Each weekend he taught the new believers.

It was quite a sacrifice to leave his wife and children and cycle seven miles into the bush in the hot sun. When I met him in Jinja and heard what he was doing, I asked him, 'Can I come with you some time?'

'Do you really want to?' was his response.

I assured him I was ready to cope with the living conditions. I had never stayed in a mud house yet and was eager to enter into what God had said.

It was great to share this experience with Liz, one of my best friends. We had known each other since we were in Sunday school together at the age of seven. Despite going our separate ways, our paths had crossed several times – at school, college and work. She had been a member of Praise with a Vision, which had drawn us closer together. Liz went out to the mission field before me: three months in St Lucia and then nine months in Kinshasa, Zaïre. I knew she would adjust easily to the culture and lifestyle here. She kept commenting on the differences between Zaïre and Uganda. 'The Ugandans seem more gracious and orderly,' she remarked. And her blue eyes grew wide as she admired the abundance of fruit and vegetables in the market.

What a sight we must have been, cycling into the bush. We caused a stir among the locals whose small houses lined the bumpy, narrow dirt track we were on. Soon everyone knew that there were two *muzungus* going to preach in Nawampendo.

'Hey, Ant!' shouted Liz as her bike overtook mine on a wider stretch of path. 'My back's not hurting at all!'

'Praise the Lord!' I responded.

Even healthy backs might have suffered on such a jerky ride. The sun beat down heavily on us. The loose steering on my bike made it difficult to stay out of the ruts in the track, especially with someone on the back. But we persevered and for the last mile, we walked and let the sweat dry on our weary bodies.

'Aren't you afraid of coming so deep into the bush?' one pastor asked me.

'Afraid of what?' I replied indignantly. God was with us so what on earth was there to fear? In fact I loved it. This was what made my heart soar. I loved the countryside, the fresh air, the animals, the plants and trees. Little old ladies sat peacefully by the side of the road making grass mats to sell, while others sold jackfruit, pawpaw, delicious juicy pineapples and sweet bananas.

At around 4.00 p.m. we arrived, happy but exhausted. We sat on a wooden bench in the shade of the mud house where we would spend the night. We enjoyed a cool drink of passionfruit juice made with boiled water stored in a beautifully shaped clay pot which they call the 'African fridge'. The water had a kind of smoky flavour which I rather liked.

People started to arrive for the meeting. Mats were laid down on the ground under a tree for them to sit on. Women carried their babies on their backs, and men wearing freshly washed shirts came eagerly to listen. The pastor opened the meeting and Johnson introduced us to the people. Liz shared a scripture and I preached a short message on the vine and the branches from John 15. Johnson challenged the people to believe God to work miracles in their lives.

After a candlelit supper round a local wooden table, Liz and I went into our little room. We shared a narrow bed, the only one they had. I looked at the mud walls and thatched roof. This was hard to believe.

'Where's the toilet?' Liz asked.

'Walk behind the house, towards the banana trees, past the cow . . .'

'What happens if the cow moves?' Liz squawked.

We rolled on the bed laughing, until the words finally came out of my mouth: 'It's tied up.'

Oh dear! We had come to that stage where everything seems funny. A missionary friend of mine called it 'night-nurses' euphoria'. The others in the house must have wondered what all the noise was about.

We didn't sleep much that night, partly through excitement and partly because we kept eating each other's hair. Liz's blonde hair almost reached her waist and I found her ponytail wrapped round my neck more than once that night.

The next day we preached again and Jesus healed people and filled them with His Holy Spirit. An Anglican vicar came to see us. He had been seeking the infilling of the Holy Spirit for a long time. I was blessed by his humility as he and his wife knelt on the mat while we laid hands on them. They certainly received, and not exactly in a quiet way! We then baptised a few of the new believers in the murky waters of a small waterhole surrounded by grass and reeds.

Back at the house we were served with delicious food. The lady was sorry they could not give us chicken, the normal visitor's treat and the most expensive meat in Uganda. One of the children had let the chicken out of the pen and someone missed the meeting chasing the poor thing, unable to catch it. So we were served with delicious beans and the best *matooke* I had ever eaten. This is the staple food of Uganda, made from peeled savoury bananas steamed in a big banana leaf over charcoal, and always eaten with a sauce.

The time came for us to leave. We set off on bikes back to Iganga for another mission. Despite the lightning and rumbling thunder we kept cycling, but soon it pelted with rain and we ran for shelter into a school building.

'Where's my sweatshirt?' asked Johnson. I had been using it to pad the metal bars of the bike seat.

'Oh no! Maybe it fell off in the rush to get out of the rain,' I yelled, running back outside to look for it on the path. But it had already disappeared.

Inside an empty classroom, I wrung out my drenched clothes and lay flat on a hard, wooden bench, praying for strength. The rain subsided and we set off, but after a few minutes it poured down again and we found a house hidden behind a coffee plantation and several cassava bushes. We took refuge on the terrace. I stood there, arms folded, throwing my weight on to one leg and then the other, trying to get warm. Lizzie smiled at me, reading the words on my T-shirt which said: 'No Hurry in Africa!' It was a gift from an American missionary in Burundi. I had simply said it was nice and he took it off and gave it to me!

A little girl came out of the house, looking rather shy. Then another child came, and soon about four more appeared. I hadn't realised I had been humming one of the Luganda praise songs until they all joined in at full volume, singing enthusiastically and enjoying the music. Those children had rhythm. We were struck by such talent hidden away in a remote place. When they stopped singing, I greeted them in Luganda and asked, *'Muli balokole?* Are you saved?' They all nodded. I crouched down and asked the little one, *'Oyagala Yesu?* Do you love Jesus?'

'Ye nnyabo, yes madam,' he answered in a cute voice.

'Aaah,' Liz and I said simultaneously. They sang a few more songs until the rain stopped, and we went on our way refreshed.

At Iganga taxi park we hired a car and a driver to take us

along a slightly better road to Namongalwe. Liz couldn't resist taking a photo of Johnson sitting in the rusty vehicle with its shattered windscreen. On arrival we walked straight to the church, a small building with mud walls, a mud floor and a thatched roof. The pastor, Andrew Mutengu, was full of Holy Ghost fire. He led the people in worship which was as good as anywhere else in the world, and yet we were in the middle of nowhere with no electricity and the only instrument being goatskin drums. These people loved Jesus and we felt immediately at home.

For the few days we were there, we all ministered. One time, the presence of God came down so strongly, Johnson had to stop preaching. Never before had I felt God's nearness so tangibly. All we could do was worship. One lady prophesied, shouting out my name: 'Anthea, Anthea, I'm sending you on a mission. Fear not, I am with you. You will heal the sick. I'm sending you on a mission.' Another woman tried to run out, afraid of what was happening. As she reached the door, the Holy Spirit arrested her and she fell down, lying there for some time while God dealt with her.

We prayed for those who were ill and many were touched by the power of the Holy Spirit. One lady screamed, arms and hands trembling in the air. She fell over and rolled on the dusty floor. Although I didn't feel afraid, I wasn't quite sure how to handle these demonic manifestations. I watched Johnson to see what he would do. 'Come out!' he shouted firmly. There was a struggle and then the lady settled down and came back to her senses. 'They have to obey Jesus,' Johnson said. I enjoyed watching him in operation. He quietly prayed throughout the day, constantly giving to people. His lifestyle was one of sacrificial service to God and I drew from his wisdom, particularly concerning ministry.

We spent most of the day in the church, but I had a chance to walk around the village, down the winding paths leading to people's mud houses. It was easy to tell people about the Lord. I sat on some locally made stools with one man who spoke English. He called the rest of his family to sit on mats on the ground and I shared about the love of God with the family. My original aim for the walk was to find a mango, but God had prepared a different work.

While we were in Namongalwe, we stayed in a brick house which had a tile roof. Liz and I shared a room. One pane of glass was missing, and I pulled the curtain to the edge of the window so the sunlight would not wake us up. We certainly needed a good night's sleep.

In the morning, I wandered out early to get a drink of water.

'How did you sleep?' asked Johnson pointedly.

'Great!' I replied.

'Really?' he questioned. 'Some thieves came in the night trying to steal the electricity wires. Didn't you hear anything?'

'No, I slept deeply,' I told him.

'You know the night guard who sat on the steps outside with a gun?' he continued. 'Well, when the thieves started shooting he got excited and also fired into the air. Twenty-nine bullets flew over the roof – and you mean you didn't hear?' he asked in disbelief.

'No,' I said shaking my head.

'How about Liz?'

'I think she slept through it, too.'

'If she didn't hear, don't tell her,' Johnson instructed. 'She'll be frightened.'

I went back into the room where Liz was waking up. 'How did you sleep?' I asked her.

'Like a log,' she replied sleepily.

'Good,' I said and kept quiet.

I could hardly believe Johnson's story was true, but I was convinced when I noticed that our curtain had been moved back in the night. Someone had put their hand through the window from the outside. It was only when we left the village that we told Liz the whole story.

Back in Kampala, we went to Miracle Centre. As we approached, the noise from the church gave the impression that someone had scored a goal in a football match. The time of worship was powerful. As the singers and musicians came down from the stage a woman in a yellow dress ran to the front, pointing at the worship leader. 'You flashy man, you're just putting on a show. That was not real praise.' He stood his ground, recognising where the accusation came from. Others in the congregation shouted at the demon, commanding it to go, and the woman was carried off, screaming and fighting. This was a common occurrence, especially after a powerful move of God. I admired the way the men of God reacted when this happened. A calm, fearless authority was demonstrated.

A woman came on to the stage and began to speak. 'I received Christ ten days ago. And on Thursday my neighbour rushed to me for help. Her four-year-old son was ill. I drove them to the hospital but the car ran out of fuel, as the petrol station was still waiting to be supplied. I took my Bible in my hand and said, 'God, please supply.' The Lord filled the tank and we reached the hospital. The doctors said there was no hope and a few minutes later the little boy died.' At this point, many people in the congregation tutted in sympathy.

'We got back in the car and the Holy Spirit came on me powerfully. It felt like electricity all over me. I was compelled to drive to Miracle Centre. I picked up the boy's body and carried him into the church, commanding the life to come back into him. His eyelids fluttered and he started moving. One of the pastors ran to see what was happening. We knew God had done a miracle. And many of our neighbours and relatives have accepted Jesus as their Lord and Saviour. Hallelujah!' she shouted.

The people in the church jumped out of their places and danced around, screaming and giving their praise to God. I looked at Liz to see her reaction. 'This is the fifth story I've heard in two months of someone being raised from the dead,' I told her.

After the meeting, Liz and I had some precious moments walking along the moonlit road to the nearby market. The air was cool and fresh. We bought some very tasty tomatoes, some *mandasis* (the local doughnuts) and triangular samosas filled with spicy peas. They were delicious, particularly as we were so hungry.

Time flew by and on Liz's last night some of Johnson's friends invited us for a meal before taking us to the airport. Their big house had a balcony overlooking the city of Kampala in the distance. There were palm trees, and other greenery decorated the foreground. We sat and relaxed, listening to all the different noises. The frogs started their throaty croaking, the birds sang their last song as the sun set and the hissing crickets sounded their permanent percussion. We could hear goats bleating, dogs barking and the low hum of children's voices in the distance. We watched the city light up as dusk fell. We had fun with Justine and Richard. After a delicious supper, we prayed together, trying to stay awake until we set off for the midnight check-in.

'Oh no, Liz needs money for the airport tax,' I remembered. We had forgotten to keep some by. I had only a few shillings. Richard and Johnson dug into their pockets and Justine checked her handbag. We put our loose change together and still had less than half the amount needed. Liz was so unconcerned. 'Oh well, I'll just have to stay in Uganda,' she said when the lady behind the counter insisted that she would not be allowed on the flight without paying the tax. Justine and Richard looked anxiously at each other, lips tightly closed. In true Liz fashion, she walked directly up to a young Canadian man, sitting on the floor of the airport, his luggage sprawled out around him. 'Can you lend me some money?' she asked. She wrote out a cheque which he gladly accepted. Richard and Johnson marvelled at the way he trusted the cheque of a complete stranger. Liz and I laughed.

It was sad to say goodbye. Lizzie had brought so much joy and had been a great encouragement to me. However, I was glad I was not going back to England. There were still many more things to experience.

I decided to spend a few days resting in Kampala. I was somewhat exhausted with all the moves around the country, lack of decent sleep and people, people – lovely people; just too many at once for this privacy-lover! I put on my Ambre Solaire sun oil, which I think had psychological effects on me as the unique scent was always associated in my mind with relaxing beach holidays, and I went for a walk around the area, exploring new paths. I felt as if God was walking beside me.

I met Anna, my neighbour. She had malaria. I offered to pray for her, but she seemed reluctant. We carried on chatting and I saw pain written all over her face as she clutched her stomach.

'Come on, let's pray,' I said gently. We went into their house. 'You know, the reason why God sent Jesus to die was so that you could be made whole in every way,' I began. 'Jesus died so that you could be forgiven for all the wrong things you have ever done and thought, and He also shed His blood so that you could be healed. The Bible tells us that He took our sicknesses on Him. Jesus has already done it, so we don't have to tolerate this sickness.' Her eyes opened wide as she listened. This sounded like good news.

'Jesus accepted being whipped, and the stripe marks on His back were so that we could be healed. The Bible says, "By his stripes we are healed." '

Before I could continue, another lady butted in. She was working as a nurse in one of the hospitals in Kampala.

'I've always wanted to know how I can be saved. What does it really mean?' she asked earnestly.

I went through a few scriptures and explained as best as I could in simple English. 'You're so eager!' I exclaimed.

'There's no one else to look to. There are too many troubles. Only God can help us,' she said.

Anna and a young boy wanted to give their lives to the Lord. I encouraged them to pray their own prayer and then laid hands on them. Another lady called Miriam said she was already saved.

'I have terrible pain in my eyes,' she told me. 'I've been suffering for a long time. But once I dreamt that someone laid hands on me and I was instantly healed.'

I prayed for her and the pain left. Then I encouraged her to pray in tongues, which she did, amazing the whole household.

They boiled up some milk for *chai* (tea) and gave me a mango and some *mandasis*. Anna had gone to bed behind a curtain hanging up in the corner of the room. I noticed her baby was wearing black rubber bands on her wrists, a form of witchcraft, supposedly to protect the baby from illnesses and evil spirits. One could pay extortionate amounts to obtain such things. I told Anna that she should no longer involve herself in those practices. 'The God who created the universe has all the power necessary to protect your baby.' She agreed and I took the bands off the baby's wrists. Before I left the house, one of the others said, 'Please, come back and teach us the Word of God so we can become strong.' I was amazed at their understanding. They had such faith and determination.

The next day I visited again. Catherine, the nurse, was so excited about following Jesus. She had told her friends at the hospital. 'Are you serious?' her close friend asked her three times. 'You, of all people!'

Anna's husband was at home and I imagined he was a bit embarrassed to see me. He was a Muslim and had two wives. He thought Jesus could not possibly accept him. Now one of his wives had become born again. He had many questions. Sometimes I couldn't follow his train of thought. He said, 'I can't become a Christian because I don't have any money.' Maybe he thought he would have to give money to the church and because they were poor, he wouldn't manage. I took him through the scriptures where God promises to bless and prosper those who obey Him. 'That's all very well for the future,' the man reasoned, 'but what about now? We don't have any money for supper. Can God do that?'

'Yes,' I answered. 'The Bible tells us that whatever we ask in the name of Jesus, it shall be done. Let's pray now and ask God to supply.'

I didn't want to give them money and make them dependent on me. It was much better to teach them to trust God for themselves. Then their focus would be on the One who has limitless resources and unending love.

After praying, Anna escorted me back to my house in the usual African way. At the gate, a woman came by, carrying a tray of eggs on her head. She looked at us, stopped and brought the tray down. Taking six eggs in her hands she offered them to me. I was flabbergasted. It was normal for strangers to ask me, a white person, for money in the street, but this had never happened before. I took the eggs, gave them to Anna and we laughed. 'God heard our prayer,' we agreed. She wrapped them in a piece of cloth and walked home happily.

One time, a driver disappeared with their vehicle for five days. They thought he had gone for ever and were devastated, as this was their only source of income.

'Don't worry,' I told them, 'God will do a miracle for you. The Bible says that nothing is impossible for him who believes. So let's believe God together and pray.'

We commanded the vehicle to come back in the name of Jesus, and the next day, a miracle happened. The driver had intended to steal the vehicle but the Holy Spirit convicted him of his wrong-doing and he came back very repentant. Anna and her husband were grateful to God.

What I liked about these people was that they believed in the authority of God's Word. If the Bible said it, that was enough. And God rewarded their childlike faith.

One night, I suddenly felt hot and feverish. I went to the kitchen where Godfrey, Harriet and a few others were chatting.

'I feel really strange. What do you think it is?' I asked.

'Probably malaria,' concluded Godfrey when I explained the symptoms.

'I think you're right. I was bitten by so many mosquitoes and I forgot to take my malaria tablet yesterday,' I added.

Godfrey laid hands on my head. 'I rebuke this sickness in the name of Jesus,' he said sternly. I nearly passed out but got a grip on myself before falling over. That night I slept solidly for twelve hours, the best sleep since arriving in Uganda. In the morning I felt better, although still quite weak. I decided to travel to Jinja and be part of the next mission.

As I approached the grassy square, it was good to hear Julius' praises filling the air. The joy of Jesus was flowing out from him. He had a professional-sounding voice and had written some excellent songs, based on scripture. We loved to sing harmonies on the roof in Kampala. I almost envied the way he prayed. He seemed to be talking directly to God and one could feel His presence while listening. 'How does he do that?' I wanted to know. He had learnt to communicate with God, spirit to Spirit. Sometimes, in the West, our minds govern our prayers more than our spirits. The Holy Spirit can educate our minds to pray according to God's will.

We stayed with a lady called Margaret. She had cooked a delicious supper which I couldn't eat. I was sweating and my temperature was so high I nearly passed out. My head was throbbing. At night, rather than disturbing the three girls sleeping in the small room with me, I paced up and down in the courtyard and sat on the steps, my head in my hands. A mosquito whined past my ear and I flapped at it so it wouldn't settle. In the morning, my temperature was still high but I finally managed to sleep, despite my spinning head. Even lying on the bed, I felt as if I was floating round the room.

Johnson took me to a small clinic in town. I could hardly walk straight on the uneven paving stones. I wasn't too impressed with the doctor. 'Where's my pen?' he said, rummaging in the untidy drawer of a desk containing a mixture of thermometers, papers and other bits and pieces shoved in together. He left the room, returning five minutes later with a pen, and a tablet which he said would be enough to cure me. Back at the house I was greeted by

Margaret, who was a nurse. She took one look at the tablet.

'Oh no! You mustn't take that. Let me give you these.' She opened a cabinet and brought out five different sorts of tablets, of varying colours.

'Who should I trust, Lord?' I prayed.

Noticing my reluctance, Margaret explained that the tablet the doctor had given me was a very strong drug, only for those who had suffered from malaria many times and did not respond to other medication. The side-effects could have been horrendous.

'So what are all these for?' I asked with a sigh. I was not used to taking tablets. It was uncommon for me to take even a Disprin. I normally preferred to pray, thinking that one day I might have to rely purely on God. That was just something personal God taught me. Thankfully I've been blessed with good health throughout my life, for which I am very grateful. Margaret explained what each tablet was for and I dutifully swallowed them at regular intervals throughout the day.

I couldn't work out whether the 'drunk' feeling was because of the drugs or the malaria. My sweat had the most strange smell and my clothes were dripping. After two days, I started to feel a bit better, but my vision was very jumpy and I could see swirling white spots, a most weird sensation. It felt as if I was not quite on earth. Margaret assured me it would wear off.

I found enough strength to preach at a seminar session. I had come to Jinja with a sense of what God wanted to do and up until then I had not been involved. A Frenchman came to the meeting hall to see what was happening. He was touring Africa and had suffered with stomach problems. He agreed to let me pray for him, so I laid my hands on him and rebuked the sickness. The next day, he came back happily. 'My stomach's fine now.' I spent time telling him about the Lord, but he was full of his own philosophies. He liked a good discussion and recognised that God had touched him but he was not ready to put his life in God's hands.

In the crusade I sang on stage with the other praise leaders. People were amazed to see a *muzungu* singing all the Luganda songs and dancing Ugandan style. The praise took off and I thoroughly enjoyed myself, but I felt it wise to go back to the house rather than sit through the preaching.

The next day I was greeted by a skeleton of a Johnson. I was shocked. How could he suddenly have become so thin? It was malaria and typhoid. Margaret gave him two injections and I hired two *boda-boda* bikes. These are a common form of public transport in certain towns in Uganda. The *boda-boda* men earn a living by carrying people from place to place all day in the hot sun. Women sit side-saddle, sometimes with a baby or child, and men sit astraddle.

'You don't need to come,' said Johnson, thinking of the expense.

'You're not going on your own,' I insisted and jumped on the back of my bike. It was dark by now and I held on tight, praying that we wouldn't go down any potholes, as the driver sped off. Suddenly I heard a scuffling noise. We came alongside the other bike and I saw Johnson's legs dragging along the ground.

'Stop!' I shouted to the man. Johnson had passed out and collapsed on the driver.

I jumped off my bike and held on to Johnson, who was draped over the handlebars, still unconscious.

'Did he explain where he lives?' I asked.

'Yes, we know roughly,' they replied, and we set off in that direction. As we entered his road, Johnson came back to consciousness and pointed to the house. We helped him on to the bed and I laid hands on him and prayed. A nine-year-old boy agreed to sleep there for the night. He kept his eye on Johnson and prayed for him. I went back that night and interceded seriously, crying tears to God. No way could this man of God die. The next day, I made some juice from passionfruit and freshly squeezed oranges and walked the fifteen-minute journey to his house, jug in hand. He was feeling much better that morning and I was so relieved.

I enjoyed spending time on the golf course near the source of the Nile. The river majestically leaves Lake Victoria, winding its way northwards through the desert, giving life wherever it goes. Many people believe that this river is a parable about Uganda. God is sending out missionaries to take His power and love to the dry and thirsty nations of the world. The Ugandans, who have persevered in the face of suffering, are being equipped and anointed by God for the task.

In Kampala, Harriet gave me a great welcome. She had missed me. 'You know, Anthea? God has done something good for me,' she began. 'I've been serving God here for eight years, cooking and cleaning for the men of God. But recently I have felt so, so bad; I thought I would die. Everyone was against me, even the people I love and pray for. And I gave up praying and reading the Bible. I was exhausted. Then when you came, you loved me and encouraged me. God has lifted me up and now I'm free. I don't know what would have happened if you hadn't come,' she continued. 'I felt I was going to die. I wanted to run away but where would I go? God sent you here just for me,' she concluded.

I felt so content inside. What a privilege it was to serve God, to bind up the broken-hearted and set the captives free.

'You know, Harriet, whenever you humble yourself and serve so faithfully, in His time, God will lift you up. He has a great plan for you and the good seeds you have been sowing will soon produce a harvest.'

My last mission was in Entebbe. I stepped on to the grass and walked towards the neatly placed benches in the shade of the building opposite. There was no church building, so it was in the open air. A few people sang and danced while others arrived.

I was not expecting to teach during the first meeting, but they called me forward and I knew they wanted me to speak. I started talking about cultivating praise and thanksgiving as a lifestyle and the power that can be released as a result. I looked around the crowd. Many of these people were well educated. They valued the teaching. I prayed for about twenty-five people for various needs they had. It was wonderful to sense God's Spirit being released.

Afterwards we walked back to the pastor's house in the dark, avoiding the many bikes coming from all directions with no lights and often no brakes. They didn't seem to care if there was a pedestrian on the road. As there were no pavements it was necessary to keep one's ears open and jump out of the way at regular intervals. The lake flies must have thought my mouth was a reservoir, the number that kept flying in. So we resorted to silence, making our way past the smells of rotting rubbish and chicken roasted on charcoal by the roadside.

The house was lit by candles as there was no electricity that evening. Milly, Pastor Charles' wife, showed me to my room. There were two beds. I pressed the mattress to see how comfortable it was. 'Yes, I think I can sleep here,' I thought aloud. But had Milly really said I would be sharing this room with a brother? Maybe that was a language error, as 'he' was often used instead of 'she' because there was no difference in Luganda. I sat on the bed and leant down to open my bag – and saw a pair of men's shoes under the bed opposite. Then my male room-mate walked in, so I disguised my shock and adjusted to the idea, which wasn't as terrible as I had thought. We lay on our beds and spoke about the Lord and then prayed together before going to sleep.

The next morning, Charles took me to a hotel and paid for me to have a swim, leaving me there while he travelled to Kampala. I felt almost guilty sitting on the sunbed writing the scriptures for the afternoon's teaching session. This is what I had been missing – peace and quiet and relative privacy. What a relief it was to my weary mind and body. The only problem was that I had no sun cream with me. The people in the teaching seminar must have wondered why my face was bright red. They were not distracted for long, as they settled down to digest the teaching on prayer.

The next morning I went for a walk along the road. It was cool after the rain. A man shouted rudely, '*Muzungu!*' The term was not normally used derogatively, but I didn't like this man's attitude. Another man brushing his teeth, leaning up against the cracked wall of the house, shouted in English, 'You! Where are you going?'

My instant reaction was to shout back, '*Gwe! Ogendawa?* You! Where are you going?' in the same gruff tone of voice he had used. They looked shocked. The woman peeling *matooke* nearly fell off her stool. I walked on quickly, trying to conceal my laughter.

'Who taught you Luganda?' they yelled, as I disappeared down the lane. I kept on walking, but when I returned I just smiled and waved. Their attitude had changed; they treated me with respect because I knew some of their language.

In Kampala I tried to extend my ticket so I could accompany Godfrey and Fiona on their trip to Tanzania. After sending many faxes to the UK and waiting for replies, I realised it was not possible, so I confirmed my flight and prepared to leave. On the morning of my departure, Robert Kayanja returned.

'I'm leaving this evening,' I told him.

'No,' he said, shaking his head.

But there was no choice. I had already tried to change my ticket, with no success.

I gave away some of my remaining possessions, and zipped up my suitcase. Packing was never a time-consuming problem to me. Out of nowhere, I heard a low rumbling sound and felt the room shaking slightly.

Five people ran into my room. 'Did you hear that? Did you hear that?' they clamoured.

'What?'

'How do you say it in English? Earth . . .'

'An earth tremor?' I suggested.

'Yes.'

'Oh, I thought it was the fridge making its usual noise,' I said, giggling.

Godfrey hired a minibus to take me to the airport for my midnight flight. I felt happy as we travelled, the vehicle packed to full capacity with singing people.

'When will you be back?' they asked.

'I don't know – God knows,' was my short reply before I disappeared behind the swinging doors.

6

Go into all the World

*Childlike trust is the backbone which enables
you to stand. Active faith, the muscles which
enable you to move*

'Wow, what an adventure!'

'Yeah,' said Jan, always ready to agree enthusiastically.

'I wonder how many countries we'll actually manage
to visit,' I pondered as we leaned over the large map of
Africa. 'Where's Zimbabwe? Oh, there it is. I think we
should start in Kenya and work our way round. Tickets
are cheaper for flights there.'

I had been to see Colin Urquhart immediately after arriving back from Uganda.

'I was discussing with Dan Chesney about sending someone to Africa to visit the ex-Roffey students from the last five years,' Colin said. 'How about it?'

'Well, yes. Sounds great, but I wouldn't be happy to go on my own,' I responded.

'Who would you want to go with you?' Colin asked.

'Well I'd love it if Jan could come, but I don't know whether you could release her from the kitchen work.'

'Leave it with me and we'll see how the Lord sorts it out.'

Very soon Jan and I were planning, praying and writing to all the people we wanted to visit. At that time I was not aware how unreliable the post can be in Africa. Later I discovered how much God had honoured our faith.

With excitement, Jan and I boarded the plane. We had no itinerary and no definite schedules. But we were ready to go through all the doors that God would open. At Nairobi Airport, we recognised Meshack Maina. He took us in a taxi through the busy streets of Nairobi to find a *matatu* (public transport vehicle). For more than an hour we sat motionless in the crowded van, waiting for other passengers to arrive. Finally we set off on the beautiful route, descending into the Rift Valley. Our hearts were bursting with praise and thanksgiving.

In the town of Nakuru, we boarded another crowded *matatu* which bumped its way along a dirt road to the remote village of Elementeita. When we got off the bus, a lady ran out of a mud house, followed by two girls. It was Grace, Meshack's wife, and their two daughters, Bernice and Mary. Beaming with joy, she hugged us both. I had never received such a welcome in my life before, especially not from a stranger. But these were no strangers.

We had found some dear brothers and sisters in Christ. Not only did they open their home to us, but their hearts as well.

We entered the house and prayed together, thanking God for the safe journey and dedicating our stay into His hands. We were shown to our little room containing a four-foot bed and a small table where we could place our cases. There was not much space for anything else. 'Close fellowship tonight!' I said to Jan, laughing.

The walls and floors were made of mud but the house was kept spotlessly clean and tidy throughout our seven-week stay. Whenever it rained, the water ran off the tin roof into two barrels and was used for cooking and washing dishes and clothes. Separate from the house stood a little hut with a tin roof where we washed in a bowl of water. The latrine was next door.

The air gently bathed our faces and the breeze ruffled Jan's long blonde hair as we admired the scenery. We looked at each other, shaking our heads. Wild zebras grazed a short distance away from the house and gazelles strutted along with their stripy tails held high as if they owned the land.

'Hey Jan,' I said, breaking the silence. 'Aren't those mountains in the background beautiful with their blue-green ridges?'

'Oh yes,' she agreed, gazing into the distance. The singing of different types of birds could be heard and the occasional whizzing of a fly as it passed. It was very soothing. We breathed the clean air deeply. This was Africa. The view in every direction was worth a photo.

Elementeita was a small village, yet there were more than three churches.

'Why don't they just join together?' I asked Meshack innocently.

'They can't,' he replied, shaking his head. 'They're from different denominations.'

As we prayed, Jan and I sensed a religious spirit pervading Kenya. As time went on, we found this to be true. We heard of church splits over petty issues. The concept of the universal Church, the Body of Christ, had penetrated into the hearts of few people. Many Christians felt unworthy and lived under a sense of false condemnation, without experiencing the cleansing power through the blood of Jesus. I wondered what kind of spiritual food they were given from the pulpit. The spiritual health of the people is always a reflection of the Church's teaching. They needed to be built up in faith with scriptures that speak of what God has done for them. Maybe some had been sitting under what I call 'bee-in-the-bonnet' preaching, where the preacher gets worked up about a particular issue that bothers him rather than enabling the people to enter into the freedom of the sons of God. Jesus instructed Peter, 'Feed my lambs.' He didn't say, 'Nag my lambs'!

I sensed that God would do something special on this trip. In the natural, I felt inadequate for the task up ahead. But I was encouraged that God knew the gifts He had given me, and my level of experience and maturity. He had sent me, believing I was the right person for the job. My confidence was in Him. I didn't need to seek some new revelation or borrow someone else's teaching. I simply needed to share what was real in my life. If I was not living it, others would not grasp it. But whatever was demonstrated in me could be reproduced in them.

Every day in the church, people gathered for praise and teaching. The Kenyan style of singing was completely different from the Ugandan music. The interesting sounds and harmonies of the Kikuyu songs were accompanied by the beating of a thin, round drum, three inches deep and about twenty inches in diameter. It was made from a type of skin and was strapped to the shoulder and beaten loudly with a stick. If two drums were being played, the noise was amazing. The singing was almost deafening even without a PA system.

Jan's main aim was to be a support to me, and she certainly was. It was so good to have a friend to laugh and pray with; I could understand why Jesus sent the disciples out two by two. I did most of the preaching. While I prepared messages, she spent time with people, sharing the love of Jesus, often in very practical ways. We both spent a morning harvesting maize with Grace and her sister Lea.

Meshack organised ministry each weekend in the churches he was overseeing in different villages. One Friday at 11.00 a.m. we carried our bags to the roadside and sat in the shade of a wooden bus shelter. Sometimes only two or three vehicles would pass in the morning. We would watch the clouds of dust approaching from a distance. When the vehicle came nearer we could see if it was a *matatu* or a private vehicle. Quite often we waited two or three hours for transport into Nakuru.

The *matatu* finally came. It swayed about dangerously, avoiding ruts in the road. Something touched me from behind. Often children liked to feel our unfamiliar hair. I turned and saw a drunk man trying to catch my hair which was blowing in the wind. Then he threw up and Jan and I moved to the front of the vehicle.

The cold, wet weather in Dundori took us by surprise. It was so different from the hot days and cool, dry nights in Elementeita. We slept in separate beds in a wooden house. I put a sheet inside my sleeping bag and covered myself with a blanket. In the night, I curled up in a desperate attempt to keep warm.

'Jan, are you awake?' I whispered.

'Mmm,' she mumbled.

'I'm frozen.'

'Oh you poor chicken,' she said. 'Shall I come into your bed?'

'Yes please,' I replied. We giggled so much that Meshack and Grace who were sleeping the other side of the wooden 'wall', woke up.

'Is everything all right?' they asked and we laughed all the more. But after a few minutes we fell asleep.

It rained so much that weekend and there were no tarmac roads, so walking to the church was quite an experience. Grace linked arms with me on one side and Jan on the other and we slipped around in the mud in our inadequate shoes. Reaching the church I had acquired a kilo of mud on each foot and my legs were splattered with dirt, but nobody seemed to mind about the state of the preacher. They just wanted the Word.

While walking for some relaxation we were followed by some people. 'What are you doing here?' they asked. We told them why we had come and then prayed with a group of young men who wanted to accept Jesus. On the Sunday they were baptised in the nearby lake. The church members marvelled at how God had moved.

It seemed that Kenyans were not so eager to hear the gospel. Maybe this was because their lives were reasonably comfortable. The Ugandans had been confronted with the reality of death during the war and had learnt to pray earnestly in secret because churches were closed and meetings prohibited. Persecution strengthened the Church and made unbelievers responsive to the gospel.

We returned happily to Elementeita and visited church members in their homes, with Meshack's assistant, Paul Wanganga. People would greet us by saying, '*Bwana asifiwe! Jina langu ni Mary. Nime okoka. Nampenda Yesu kama mwokozi wangu.* Praise the Lord! My name is Mary. I am saved. I love Jesus, my Saviour.' Then they would share something the Lord was doing in their lives. We rather liked this tradition, particularly when the person really meant what they were saying rather than speaking out of habit. We soon learnt enough Kiswahili phrases to be able to greet them in the same way.

When we entered one house, the whole family came to greet us, shaking our hands warmly. We were shown to some wooden seats padded with sponge cushions, a common type of chair found in a good mud house. The mother disappeared through a door and we sat quietly, wondering what was happening, enjoying the peace and the coolness after being in the hot sun. The wooden shutter of the window was open, allowing the air to flow through. About half an hour later, the lady reappeared carrying a tray of milky tea in metal cups. She placed it on the wooden table in front of us and went out again.

'Urr, it's so sweet,' said Jan.

'Yeah, they've put the sugar in already,' I said. 'Just think, she probably had to milk the cow, light the firewood and then boil the milk.'

'Do you think there's any water in it?'

'I don't think so,' I replied. 'They think of us as special visitors so they give us what they consider to be the best. They boil the milk, the tea leaves and the sugar together in one large metal pan, resting it on three stones with the firewood burning underneath.'

'Where's that lady gone now?' I asked. 'I wanted to talk to her.'

'I don't know. It seems strange that the women disappear leaving us to speak to the men,' Jan commented.

While I was still talking, I felt something pulling at my

hair. I looked round and found myself face to face with a goat poking his head in the open window. 'He must have been hungry!' I said. The children outside broke into a smile once they realised I had seen the funny side. They came and taught us to count in Kiswahili. They wondered why we couldn't speak their language and they laughed at our mistakes, but stayed patiently with us until we had mastered one to ten.

The lady returned with a plate of boiled chicken pieces and some meat juice in two cups. Jan and I looked at the oil floating around in it, thinking the same thing. 'They even killed a chicken for us. Well, praise God, we're not going to starve in this village.'

After eating as much as we could, we were taken into a dark room where an old lady lay on a mat. 'She's been sick for a long time,' our hosts explained. 'Can you pray for her?' Paul interpreted for us. I bent down beside the lady, trying to see her face in the dark. I spoke to her about the power of Jesus Christ and His suffering on the cross for each of us. I could see she was responding. When I felt she had her faith focused in the right direction, I laid hands on her and prayed, rebuking the sickness and commanding it to leave in the name of Jesus. We left her and went back into the sitting room to pray with every-body before walking back to our temporary home.

'I really sensed God's presence when you spoke to that woman,' said Jan.

'Praise God!' I said, pleased at what He was doing.

One day we walked for two hours along a dust track where few vehicles passed. The road stretched for miles across flat, dry land spotted with flat-topped trees and gorse bushes. We could see the clouds unloading rain across the valley, thankfully not on us. As we neared our destination, the terrain became slightly hilly and the vegetation changed. We passed a beautiful rocky place.

'Look at that strange tree, Jan. It's not even a tree; it's a giant cactus,' I said as we admired the plant towering twenty feet above us.

When we arrived in the village, people were waiting for us in the mud church. I felt so excited to be preaching. It seemed effortless. God was there, and the words flowed. I gave a few words of knowledge and prophecies and the sick were healed. I sensed the love of God in my heart for those precious people.

After the meeting, we went to the pastor's house and enjoyed sponge cake and thick, milky Kenyan *chai* which gave us some energy for our return journey. We set off in the dark; there was no moon. Jan held the torch and walked with the others while I lagged behind to thank the Lord for what He had done that evening. Every now and again, the others heard, 'Splash! Splash!' as I stepped in some puddles in the dark. 'Sorry!' Meshack would shout in sympathy. I found that expression amusing at first, as in England we only say sorry when it's our fault.

We made slow progress in the dark and arrived home late. Jan and I went into our little room and Bernice brought in the gas lamp and placed it on a stool.

'Hey, there's something in our room!' I shouted, hearing a sound coming from my suitcase. Jan shone the torch just in time to see a large frog leaping around among my clothes. We squealed and Grace popped her head round the door. She went out, returning with a local broom made of fine twigs bound together at one end. She waved it around where the frog was and it jumped on to the floor.

'Don't hurt him!' I shouted. 'God created that ugly creature!' Grace chased it out of the room.

'And don't come back any more, you frog,' said Jan.

'Oh the life of a missionary,' I said, stretching my weary body and falling on to the bed.

We met some friends of Meshack's called Chris and Patricia who were managing part of a large farm. They took us in a pick-up to their house. We enjoyed the journey. Zebras raced across our path and baboons could be seen in the fields.

'Oh look, is that a giraffe?' Jan asked.

'Where? I can't see it.'

As we drew nearer, we saw the outline more clearly. It was a man on a bike.

We passed a large tree where there were probably over a hundred monkeys. When we stopped the pick-up, they were frightened and came running down. 'I thought they would have felt safer up in the tree,' I commented.

We saw other animals too: the small rock hyrax, guinea fowl, a jackal which looked like a fox and many warthogs, which eat roots with their snouts like a pig but are a different shape and dark grey in colour.

Chris and Patricia had a lovely garden with freshly mown grass, roses and brightly coloured bougainvillaea. There were little round houses for the servants. Jan placed her camera on a wall and set the timer, allowing her to join Paul and me, standing ready for the photo. She ran towards us, jumping over a flower bed, thinking she wouldn't make it in time.

'Help!' she shouted.

The house boy rushed outside with a disconcerted look on his face and a knife in his hand.

'It's OK!' I yelled and we all laughed as the camera took the action photo.

After a few weeks of ministry, we had some free days and decided to see someone whose post office box address we'd been given. It was a friend of a friend working at a mission school and it seemed like a good adventure.

We travelled in two *matatus* to the town where the post office box was, and asked directions from there. 'The school is twenty-five kilometres down a very bad track where few vehicles go,' someone told us. Tired and thirsty from the journey, we had a drink in a local cafe while considering our next move. 'Excuse me, does anyone here speak English?' I asked, realising how foreign I was in such an environment. Some people looked away like proud cats. One man seemed a little more co-operative.

'English?' I asked.

The man shook his head.

'Kisarian School?' I said.

'Lake Baringo,' was his reply, motioning with his arms as if his hand was a boat on water.

'*Asante, asante*, thank you, thank you,' I said politely, shaking the man's hand.

'So it looks as if we should make our way to the lake and find out where to go from there,' I told Jan. We caught a bus and arrived at the lakeside as the day was drawing to a close. We managed to find a lodging place for £1.50. The room was clean but rather bare apart from two beds.

'Let's go on a hippo hunt,' I suggested.

'Yeah, we might even see a crocodile,' said Jan.

'As long as it's not too close.'

We locked our bags in our room and walked for almost an hour along the shore. The cloud formation was magnificent as the sun set, painting a sparkling orange line across the water. We saw no wild animals, but a few interesting birds with long, pointed beaks.

'There are so many mad people wandering about here,' Jan commented.

'Yes, isn't it a shame that the devil has such a stronghold in a beautiful place like this,' I thought out loud. The environment indicated that there was a lot of witchcraft. 'I wonder what the Church is doing here,' I said to Jan.

'Lord, bring Your people here to make an impact and break these strongholds in this area,' we prayed in agreement.

We found a local eating place, a little wooden shack. We stunned the locals; white people were not usually seen in such a place. The mama serving was very warm and friendly and spoke to us in Kiswahili.

'*Ugali?*' she asked with a smile. This was the staple food in Kenya; cornflour mixed with boiling water to form a thick cake of white, steaming starch to which was added some kind of meat or vegetable sauce.

'*Hapana,*' I declined, laughing. Although we ate it sometimes, our stomachs did not appreciate such food late at night. 'Chapatti?' I suggested. The lady nodded, indicating that she could serve them.

The man next to me was eating a bowl of *sukuma weeki*, a kind of dark green spinach which both Jan and I found delicious. The literal meaning of the name is 'pushing the week'. The individual leaves can be picked, leaving the plant to continue growing. It's a cheap food which can be eaten until more money comes at the end of the week. We ordered *sukuma weeki* and the woman went back into the smoky kitchen, bringing us the food half an hour later.

We chatted with the man sitting beside us. He was well educated and spoke good English. He told us he was a born-again Christian, and we were thankful to meet a brother in such a rough place.

'We're trying to get to Kisarian School. Do you know exactly where it is and how we can get there?' I asked the man.

'It's the other side of Lake Baringo, quite some distance away,' he told us. 'It may be possible to hire a boat.'

'And roughly how much do you think that would cost?' I asked.

We had to be careful with our finances and the price he suggested was too much. 'We don't have enough money,' I said, sounding disappointed. Having travelled all this way I didn't like the idea of giving up and returning to Elementeita.

'Well, that's the price for the tourists, but if you go to the Government Fisheries and negotiate with them, they may take you for less.'

'Well, thanks for your help,' said Jan gratefully. 'We'll go and see them tomorrow.'

We slept well and in the morning Jan wandered out to find some water to wash in. 'There's a kind of shower,' she told me when she returned, her long hair dripping wet. I followed her directions and went into a little wooden hut, shutting the door behind me and securing it by twisting the bent nail across the door. I turned the tap and water pelted on me from a pipe. I had just finished soaping myself when the water stopped abruptly. I looked at the pipe: nothing was coming out so I wrapped my *gitenge* cloth as a substitute towel round my soapy body and went outside. Looking back at the little wooden hut I noticed a barrel on the roof.

'Jan, the water's run out,' I said entering our room. 'Did you see where it was coming from? There's a barrel on the roof. Gravity is a wonderful thing.'

We headed towards the lake and met a friendly lady on the way.

'Hello, is this the way to the Government Fisheries?' I asked.

'Come with me. I'll show you where it is,' she said, and we walked together. During our conversation we discovered she was a strong believer in Jesus.

The lady introduced us to the manager as two preachers from England who needed help to get across the lake.

'Preach to me, I need to be saved,' he told us.

I questioned him to see where he was spiritually and then spoke about the claims of the Lord Jesus Christ. He consented to everything mentally but was not ready to surrender his life to the Lord. However, he provided us with a boat and driver.

The water was still and smooth and the breeze was refreshing in the hot sun. After forty-five minutes we arrived. The school really was in the middle of nowhere. Our friend's friend seemed surprised to see us. We spent some time talking and had a meal with two elderly South African lady missionaries who lived near the school. When we got back over the lake, we thanked the driver for patiently waiting for us.

We walked to the road. Some men sat outside a wooden shack, playing draughts using a piece of cardboard and some bottle tops.

'Hello. How are you?' I said.

'Yes, we're fine. How are you?' they answered. 'We're fine,' I said, following the system.

It is not acceptable in Africa to speak before greeting properly, so we learnt how to gain favour with the people rather than offend them. Even in shops, especially in rural areas, it is considered rude not to acknowledge an assistant before she serves you.

'Can you help us?' I asked. 'We're looking for transport back to Marigat.'

The men laughed mockingly. 'Ah, there's no transport in the afternoon hours. You'll have to sleep here.'

There was no decent hotel in that place. 'Let's believe God for a miracle,' Jan and I agreed. We sat with the men and played draughts.

Suddenly we heard the sound of a vehicle. It was a large lorry crammed full of people and schoolchildren standing up in the open back. We waved to the driver who was sitting high up in his cabin. He leant out of the window. 'Where to?' he asked.

'Marigat!' I shouted.

'If you can climb up, you can have a ride,' he said, watching for our response.

'Are you going that way?' I asked, just to make sure. It wouldn't have been the first communication breakdown I'd had.

'Yes,' he assured us.

We threw our bags up to the people standing in the back of the lorry and climbed up, placing our feet on the large tyres and hoping the vehicle wouldn't roll back at the wrong moment. When the people saw our faces, they screamed and laughed. They didn't expect white people to travel in such a way. Grabbing our arms, they pulled us up to safety. The lorry lurched and we all staggered about. People walking along the road pointed at us and yelled in amazement.

At Marigat we booked ourselves into a hotel, an oasis in that frantic town full of drunkards. After a lovely meal, we locked ourselves securely in our room, refusing to open the door to those who knocked. The atmosphere was not exactly one of safety. We were so tired. I tucked the mosquito net under the mattress and lay down, claiming the Lord's protection and peace to prevail in that noisy place.

Early in the morning we travelled to Nakuru, meeting up with Paul and Meshack. They were pleased we were back safely. We went straight to the town of Molo for a mission. The first meeting was supposed to begin that very morning. We reserved our places in the public transport minibus, and then Meshack went to look in one of the shops while I kept an eye on our luggage, standing up to stretch my aching legs.

In Kenya it was election time. There was political upheaval in the country, with rioting, campaigns and the burning of people's houses. Free food and money were distributed in exchange for votes. As I stood in the street I heard a terrible noise of shouting and screaming. Round the corner a hundred people came running straight towards me. I raced to the side door of the minibus and was shoved in by five panic-stricken people also trying to get out of danger. The minibus swayed and rocked as people's bodies bashed against the vehicle and the crowd passed.

'Where's Meshack?' Jan demanded. It was a relief when he returned a moment later from the safety of a shop.

At Molo the early meeting had been cancelled. I was pleased as there had been no time to prepare a message. The pastor treated us to chicken and chips in a cafe, after which I got a theme from the Lord for that church. I wrote down several scripture references.

'Hey Jan, this is a good verse. It's from 1 Peter 4:10–11. "Each one should use whatever gift he has received to serve others, faithfully administering God's grace in its various forms. If anyone speaks, he should do it as one speaking the very words of God." ' She nodded in agreement.

In the meeting, Meshack introduced us. Being a preacher, he found it hard to cut his words short. When he mentioned my first scripture, I was pleased for the confirmation. He continued speaking and quoted the next scripture I had written down. I showed Jan my notebook. She raised her eyebrows. When Meshack used my third scripture, I gasped. But that was not all. He quoted the fourth and the fifth scriptures I had prepared to teach on.

When he finally called me to preach I laughed and started halfway through the message, explaining that Meshack had already preached the first half.

We had a late supper and went to bed at 1.00 a.m., still tired from our previous adventure to Lake Baringo. By 10.00 a.m. we were in the church ready to preach. The singing began and I went outside for some privacy so I could hear the Lord. The house where we had stayed was very busy and there had been nowhere to go for an extended time of prayer. I walked around on the grass, looking out across the green forested hills to avoid the stares of inquisitive passers-by. God started to show me His heart for the people. I thumbed through the pages of the Bible and found the right passages opening up automatically. I knew this was God's message and not my own.

When the singing came to a close, I went back into the church. People were still arriving, dressed in their Sunday best, the little girls in frilly dresses with white below-the-knee socks and shiny patent shoes. I sat at the front next to a weary-looking Jan.

'I can see we have some visitors this morning,' the pastor began. 'Please stand up if this is your first time here.' Six people stood and one by one gave their names, where they were from and a message for the people. When the fifth person spoke for more than ten minutes, Jan looked at her watch. She sympathised with me. The message was bubbling inside as I sat, praying in tongues.

'Is this really necessary?' I whispered in Jan's ear. If the Church made more room for the Word, there would certainly be a difference in people's lives. After all, Jesus said, 'Heaven and earth will pass away, but my words will never pass away.' So, according to God, the Word has the priority.

The sixth visitor spoke on and on, complaining about

different cults emerging in Kenya, describing their customs and wicked ways in depth. It certainly did not build anyone up in faith. The whole atmosphere changed as people's minds lost their focus on God. It was not until 1.30 p.m. that I was called to preach. By this time the congregation were tired and I didn't know how much more they could take. They were eager to go home for lunch. Many times before, I had waited for two hours to preach, but this surely tested my patience. I stood up, not feeling too gracious, and inwardly praying for wisdom. I cut the message to the bare minimum, reading the main scripture, and after praying for a few people, I sat down. The pastor said how much they had appreciated the ministry and I could see from the faces of the people that they had been blessed. However, I couldn't help feeling disappointed because I sensed that God was ready to do so much more for those people, but too many hours were taken up with unnecessary and unfruitful words.

On the dusty road back to Elementeita, the poor overloaded *matatu* broke down miles from any house. I wandered along the lane, enjoying the view and the fresh air while the driver decided what to do. Two hours later, the vehicle started and we arrived back at 8.00 p.m. 'It's so good to be home,' I told Grace, pleased to be back in the peaceful environment of the village.

The next day we had a complete rest. Jan and I went for a walk, splitting up to pray in private. I returned before Jan and stood in the shade of the porch, stroking the cat who was enjoying the attention. I spotted Jan from a distance hobbling towards the house. As she drew nearer I noticed her shoelace was tied round her ankle and the side of her foot was bleeding. 'What happened?' I asked.

'I was bitten by a snake,' she replied.

'No way! How did it happen?'

'I was just stepping over a puddle on to some dry grass and a little brown snake latched on to my ankle and bit me.'

Grace sent one of the girls to find Chris's driver, who was on the farmhouse estate, twenty minutes' walk away. I prayed: 'Father, Your Word says that we shall trample on snakes and scorpions and nothing shall by any means harm us. Lord, we believe in Your promise and right now we ask for Your healing touch in Jan's body. Any poison from that snake, we cancel it in the name of Jesus. Thank You, Lord, for your healing power. Thank You, Lord, for the blood that was shed so that Jan can be healed. We bless You for the miracle You've done. Thank You, Jesus.'

'Amen,' Jan and Grace agreed.

'Well I suppose I'd still better go to the hospital,' said Jan.

Almost an hour later, the driver arrived and took us on the bumpy journey into Nakuru where Jan received two injections.

'How did you manage to get bitten by a snake?' asked the son of an English farmer. 'I've been hunting all my life, deliberately going to places where I thought I might see a snake, and I've never yet been bitten by one. But you come here for a few weeks and such a thing happens!'

The ministry was picking up in Elementeita. The people enjoyed the faith-building teaching. I heard some encouraging reports. One man called Joseph had suffered from a bad shoulder for a long time and the power of Jesus healed him. Similar testimonies were told, to the glory of God's name. One member of the church came to the house pushing his bike, carrying a heavy bucket on the rack behind. He lifted off the lid and scooped up some honeycomb in a small container, offering it to us. 'This is better than chewing gum,' I commented.

Before he was born again, this man had five wives. They lived on separate farms and each week a different wife would stay in his house with her children. When he came to the Lord, some of his wives were also born again. He managed to make two of them financially self-sufficient and remained with three wives, who often sat together in the church on the wooden benches praising the Lord happily.

Friday came and it was time for another mission. Jan had been awake all night with a bad stomach and decided to stay in Elementeita to rest. Susan, one of the church members, travelled with Paul and me to Nakuru, to meet up with Meshack at the *matatu* station. We sat on the wooden benches outside a row of kiosks where different goods were sold. After two hours there was still no sign of Meshack, so Paul put us on the *matatu* to Wanyororo, where the conference was taking place. The vehicle was a small one with two benches facing each other and a middle bar along the length of the roof. The benches were so tightly packed it seemed impossible to fit another person in, but the conductor kept trying to make more space, expecting wide-hipped ladies to squeeze into a two-inch gap. And somehow they did, as everyone shifted up. It was seriously painful for the legs. Once the benches were full, people crammed themselves in, standing bent double and holding on to the metal bar, crushed together with those in front and behind.

A lady came in with a baby on her back. She stepped up into the vehicle from the back door, untied the piece of cloth holding the baby in place and passed him to a stranger sitting in the vehicle. By now there was very little breathing space and the heat was intense. I was relieved to hear the engine start. Five young men jumped on to the back step of the moving vehicle, hanging on to the doors and the roof rack. A cartoon comic flashed into my mind as I imagined the front wheels leaving the ground. 'Lord, give us a safe journey,' I prayed earnestly.

Gradually the load lightened as people were dropped off along the way. When we reached Wanyororo, Susan looked out of the window. 'This isn't the place,' she said.

I checked with the conductor. 'Yes, this is Wanyororo,' he replied.

When Susan insisted it wasn't, the conductor suddenly remembered. 'Ah, do you want Wanyororo A or Wanyororo B?' he asked.

'Which one is this?' asked Susan.

'This is Wanyororo A,' he replied.

'So there are two places with the same name?' I exclaimed in disbelief. 'How far is the other Wanyororo?'

'Oh, very far,' said the conductor. 'You have to go back to Nakuru and get another *matatu* and travel several kilometres in the opposite direction. I tell you what, if you wait here in the vehicle while it fills up, we'll take you back to Nakuru free of charge.'

We sat in the front seat and waited for over an hour while people boarded the empty *matatu*. The driver took two wires in his hands and put them together, jerking the vehicle to a start, and we were away. At Nakuru we found the vehicle for Wanyororo B. On arriving, we were thankful to find the pastor and Meshack. The church was packed with people who had waited for us all morning. They had cooked *ugali* and *sukuma weeki* for lunch which I ate with my fingers.

I preached on overcoming Satan's tactics through the victory of Jesus, teaching from Ephesians 6 about the spiritual weapons we have. There was a real move of the Holy Spirit. People came forward for ministry and were healed. Many of them really encountered God and almost the whole congregation dedicated themselves afresh to Him.

'We didn't realise what we were missing,' one lady said when the meeting was over. 'Now we've been revived, we'll continue to pray and live by faith in God.'

The next day, we met up with Jan at Nakuru. She was feeling much better. We travelled to Njoro and arrived tired and hungry, having eaten no lunch. We went straight to an afternoon fellowship in a small house. They were a praising people and the singing was very uplifting. I prepared my message in the first half of the meeting and spoke on the character of Christ and the fruits of the Holy Spirit found in Galatians 5:22–3.

At first it seemed as if the people were not with me. I felt like shutting up and sitting down. Maybe they were not used to such teaching, or maybe they didn't like my quiet manner. I continued, asking them to pray, first of all worshipping the Lord for His character and then letting the Lord convict and empower regarding each fruit of the Spirit, praying that those fruits would be demonstrated in our lives. God was in that place in a powerful way. People were crying and repenting, not in the religious emotional manner I had seen some Kenyans do as a habit, but there was real Holy Spirit activity. It was noisy at times with everyone praying at once, so I just let it carry on. Then we walked the three kilometres back to the pastor's house in the pouring rain, still singing praises.

After a meal, Jan and I slept for a couple of hours on a small single bed. Then at 11.00 p.m. we walked to a church member's home for *kesha*, one of the regular overnight meetings which are popular in Kenya. 'I wonder if we'll manage to stay up the whole night?' I asked Jan as we trod on the spongy grass in the dark.

The meeting was very good. After others had shared, I did a short preach and led the people in prayer. It was as if we touched eternity and lost all sense of time. Before we knew it, it was already 4.30 a.m. We slept until 7.30 and then prepared for another meeting.

In the worship time, I felt I should preach on Jehovah Jireh, the Lord our Provider. I was aware of a spiritual battle. The devil was scared about what was happening. I sensed oppression among the congregation. They needed a good dose of encouragement. I sensed the heart of the pastor and some others despising me.

'Thank You, Lord, that it is no longer I who live, but Christ who lives in me. Jesus, manifest Your presence today,' I prayed silently. 'Speak Your Word to Your people and break every bondage in this place.' God had chosen me to be an instrument in His hands, whether people accepted me or not.

I enjoyed preaching that day. The people's faces changed as God brought His liberating Word to their hearts. I looked at a lady in the front row, and by the Spirit of God I knew she was feeling guilty about a grievous sin which she had already confessed to God.

'Lady, the Lord says you are free from your guilt. "I have forgiven you," says the Lord. You are now made clean. The past is gone and a new day has come for you.'

The woman fell to her knees and her large teardrops formed a puddle on the floor.

'The Lord is restoring you,' I continued. 'His blessing and favour are upon you and many will be touched by your testimony of God's unfailing love.'

Then I pointed to a man in the back row. 'Sir, do you suffer from headaches?' I asked.

'Yes,' he replied.

'Come here to the front. Jesus is going to heal you,' I

said, confident that God who had spoken would also perform the miracle. 'From this day on you will never suffer from those headaches again. Be healed in Jesus' name!' I said forcefully. He fell to the floor as the power of God came upon him.

The next few minutes continued in much the same way with different people receiving their miracles. 'How does your leg feel now?' I asked the lady I had just prayed with.

'It's fine!' she said, delighted.

'Bend it. Let's see,' I told her. 'Praise God!' I shouted, and everybody clapped to the Lord.

I prayed a final prayer of blessing on the church, took my small red Bible and sat down next to Jan. The pastor stood up in front with a strange look on his face.

'Well, we do praise God for what He has done here today,' he began in rather an unusual tone, 'but I know that if I had been the one ministering, we would have seen a lot more miracles.'

I fixed my eyes straight ahead, trying to stop my jaw from dropping open. I was shocked at this pastor's attitude.

'And as for you,' the man continued, pointing to the woman I had prophesied to, 'don't think that you're now free from our church discipline. Nobody is allowed to speak to this woman for the next six weeks. We will not tolerate her behaviour. And just because you've cried those petty tears of yours, that doesn't mean you're forgiven,' he said to her harshly.

My heart nearly broke for the woman. Like the lady caught in the act of adultery, it was the compassion of Jesus that changed her heart and her behaviour. God's kindness leads to repentance and this broken-hearted woman had been brought back to the love of Jesus. This was the Church of Jesus Christ, the One who had died for the sins of the world. Our job as believers was to bring restoration, healing and liberty to those who were bound, but the whole point had been missed and the people were being ruled and manipulated in an ungodly manner.

In the natural, there was no way I could have known the lady's situation but the Spirit of God had given me the words to speak. The Apostle Paul was accused of encouraging sin when he preached the grace and mercy of Jesus Christ and righteousness through faith. So I counted myself privileged to have experienced what I did.

Meshack, Jan and I boarded a minibus taxi. The driver free-wheeled all the way from Njoro to the outskirts of Nakuru.

'Maybe he's short of petrol,' I said.

'He's probably trying to save money,' another passenger suggested.

We returned to the safety of Elementeita. We were always assured of a good welcome and a lovely meal. We sat down by the light of the gas lamp to eat chapattis and green grams, a type of pulse which is common in Kenya. After supper, I wrote the events of the past few days in my diary, trying not to strain my eyes. I popped my head round the kitchen door. Lea, Grace and Jan were huddled together in the smoke-filled room. Lea was crouching on the floor, finishing the last of the washing-up and Jan and Grace were enjoying a joke. The cat lay near the fire to keep warm as the chill evening air descended. 'Night, night,' I said.

'*Lala salama*, sleep well,' they replied.

Our next journey was to Elburgon which took six hours. Solomon, the ex-Roffey student, was helping to pastor a church and would take over when Pastor Stephen went to Roffey in a month's time. In the church a young man

Nigeria 1990, from left to right: Francis Wale Oke, his wife,
Colin Urquhart, Anthea, Lanre Adeboye's wife,
Jonathan Croft.

Anthea and Jan baptising a young student from
Kawambwa Boys School, Zambia.

Anthea in African dress walking onto the stage at the
Abeokuta crusade, Nigeria.

Haircutting time for members of the band No Bad Thing, from left to right: Anthea, Chris Reed, Jackie Wilson, Adrian Parsons, Justine Parsons cutting Steve Fishpool's hair.

Members of the band and friends leaning on a giant tortoise, from left to right: Joseph Swaibu, Paul Williams, Chris Reed, Justine and Adrian Parsons, friend in a Minnie Mouse shirt, Stephen Drani, Justine Williams and Steve Fishpool.

Anthea preaching at an open-air crusade in Gulu, Uganda.

Anthea preaching in a Ugandan village crusade
with the help of interpreter Joyce Nantongo of the
World Wide Trumpet Mission.

On the journey from Fort Portal, West Uganda, to the
Rwenzori Mountains.

The Zambia team, from left to right: Timothy Chilufya, Anthea, Claire Hollis, Ali Parsons, Sharron Frood, Mark Robinson, Gerry George.

Children from Lukwesa, Zambia.

Bathtime at Ntumbachushi Falls, Zambia:
Anthea, Claire and Sharron.

Anthea and Sharron visiting 'Mrs Fritter' in
Kawambwa, Zambia.

Anthea being taught to read the Bible in Luganda (an African language) by orphans in Kapeeka, Uganda. Her adopted daughter, Pross, is sitting beside her on the left.

Ali, Anthea and Pastor Kakayire baptising a new convert on the shores of Sagitu Island.

introduced us. 'These are our visitors and we're going to suck all the milk from them until there's none left,' he said, snuffling at the interpreter's chest to demonstrate.

One message I preached was about the use of the tongue, speaking from James 3. 'The tongue has power to direct the course of our lives. Whenever we speak negative things, we direct our lives into those same negative things. If you call your child stupid, he will believe he is stupid, and that's what he'll become. That's the power of life and death in the tongue. God said, "Let there be light," and the light appeared. That same creative Word can be in our conversations when we say things which line up with what is in the Bible.

'Jesus said, "Be healed," and the sicknesses left. If we speak all the time about our sickness, we direct our lives deeper into the sickness, but if we speak about God's ability to heal and the blood of Jesus that makes it possible, we will direct our lives into God-given health. When we complain that we have no money, that may be a fact but it is not the truth of God's Word. The truth says that God is our Provider and if we are faithful in giving He will supply all our needs according to His riches in glory. So we need to speak along those lines and direct the course of our lives into the abundance of God.'

The people were touched by the message. Walking home in the dark that evening, Solomon told me, 'The last visiting preacher who came here three weeks ago also preached the same message.'

'This is exactly what the people need to hear,' said Pastor Stephen excitedly. 'It was such a strong, convicting message.'

'Really?' I questioned.

'Yes, it hit the target, but came across in a gentle way so people could accept it.'

Jan and I had separate beds for the first time in weeks and once again we were fed very well, with two cooked meals a day and platefuls of neatly chopped oranges and bananas. Poor Jan was still suffering with her stomach and often drank *uji*, a thin cornflour porridge, instead of eating meals.

One day, Jan went for a walk in the locality of the pastor's house, where we were staying. I stayed in the bedroom preparing my next message. Jan had only been gone for five minutes, when she suddenly burst in the bedroom door, slammed it shut and leant on it, panting breathlessly.

'What happened?' I asked her, seeing the distress on her face.

'I was followed by about twenty kids. It was OK to start with, but then they jumped up and pulled my hair. I had to run before they mobbed me. But I couldn't find the way back. These wooden fences all look the same. I just asked God to help me, because the children were catching up fast. Then I saw the gate of the pastor's house, ran through and tried to shut it, but the children pushed against it, so I raced down the garden and into the lounge where Solomon was asleep. The children followed me into the house right up to the bedroom.'

'Oh my goodness,' I said, placing a comforting hand on her shoulder.

We went into the lounge to see Solomon who had woken up suddenly, finding himself surrounded by children who refused to leave. In the end he had to chase them out of the house with a stick.

'Are you OK?' he asked Jan.

'Yes, it was just a bit of a shock,' she replied.

'One of the kids asked the pastor's little daughter, "Is that your *muzungu*?" ' Solomon told us and we laughed.

One evening I went out for a moonlight walk after

supper to pray. It was cold, so I put on a pair of cotton trousers and wrapped my *gitenge* over my head like a shawl. I soon became aware of quick footsteps behind me. I swung round. 'Attack is the best form of defence,' I thought, and directed my voice into the darkness: '*Habari?* How are you?'

I could just make out the figures of eight men who stopped in their tracks when they saw me. I heard mutterings of '*muzungu, muzungu*' and some muted discussion in Kikuyu. The men sniggered and walked away rather sheepishly.

'What was all that about?' I asked the Lord. Maybe they thought I was a prostitute looking for work, as I was wearing trousers. They had not seen my skin colour because I was covered up. Perhaps they were rushing to get to me first. I found it amusing, but the pastor was rather concerned. 'It's OK,' I assured him, 'I won't go out wearing trousers again.'

I stayed in the lounge, talking about the exciting things of God. Then for fun I started imitating their Kikuyu language.

'Hey, who taught you that?' asked Solomon.

'Taught me what?'

'You're speaking real Kikuyu. You just said the word "offspring" and then you said, "there is no problem." '

'Did I? Wow! Praise God for that,' I responded.

I went to bed but was too happy to sleep. I imagined the Lord using me to speak a whole message in Kikuyu to a congregation and ministering to individuals. That would be a pure message from Jesus with no human element involved. Jan was still awake, so I told her what had happened and we returned to the lounge. Solomon agreed to listen and he picked out several words in between unintelligible sounds.

'What have I said now?' I asked.

'You said, "Thank you" and "Lord, I want it," and then you said, "to tell you the truth".'

'Really?' I said, picking up the torch and waving it about. Then another phrase came into my mind. 'How about this one?' I spoke what I'd heard.

Solomon laughed. 'You've just said, "many torches".'

'Wow, this is amazing. I wish it would come fluently,' I told Jan.

'Keep going,' said Solomon, and I started to speak.

'Yes, you've said the word for Satan, and then you said, "enough problems" and now you've just said the word describing what's in the cow's intestines!'

I went into prayer mode and used phrases in Kikuyu such as, 'lead me' and 'sustain me completely' and I spoke of reconciliation. We thoroughly enjoyed the evening.

I went back to bed, tired but contented. I grabbed my torch and my Bible to read one more scripture for the day. I opened at 1 Corinthians 1:5–7: 'For in him you have been enriched in every way – in all your speaking and in all your knowledge – because our testimony about Christ was confirmed in you. Therefore you do not lack any spiritual gift as you eagerly wait for our Lord Jesus Christ to be revealed.'

'Thank You, Lord,' I prayed, before turning over and falling asleep.

During the next two days, God used me to speak prophetic words to people in Kikuyu as we conversed in between the meetings. Although it didn't flow fluently, people were blessed.

We went to a leaders' conference for a week in Nairobi for some input.

'Do you realise, Jan, that I've preached a minimum of six times a week for the last seven weeks? I don't feel too exhausted, but I could do with some spoon-feeding on the Word myself.'

We were a bit disappointed at the conference. There were about seven hundred church leaders and many were not born again or Spirit-filled. Some of the speakers did not seem to know the Bible very well and preferred to preach their own theories or experience. However, there were some good American preachers who spoke right into the Kenyan situation in the Body of Christ.

On Sunday, we met up with Meshack who helped us across the busy city with our large suitcases. We waited on the street checking the bus numbers as they rounded the corner.

'This one!' shouted Meshack.

We threw our heavy luggage up the steps, pushing it through the doors at the back of the bus. The other passengers stared, no one attempting to assist. Jan and I scrambled on. We climbed quickly over our luggage, heaving the cases further along the passageway to make room for Meshack. The driver pulled away just as Meshack jumped on, landing on his hands and knees. I looked at his large frame, wondering if he had hurt himself, but was relieved to see that he was laughing. 'Are you all right?' asked Jan, brushing the dust off his jacket.

'This is Nairobi,' he said goodheartedly.

We arrived at a church in a slum area and I preached twice. The message was not particularly special, but the Lord moved in an unexpected way. I called people forward to be filled with the Holy Spirit. Straight away, two girls dashed to the front and God's power knocked them out. They fell on their faces. When the others saw what was happening, more and more came forward and were baptised in the Holy Spirit. It was chaotic. The church appeared to be filling up with people and streams came forward for prayer.

'The children ran outside to bring others into the church,' Meshack told me afterwards. They had never experienced anything like it.

'Why are the people fainting?' someone asked the pastor.

A little girl brought her alcoholic father. Meshack prayed for him to receive Jesus.

The pastor took me aside at the end of the meeting. 'I became pastor of this church three months ago, and I've been preaching about the baptism of the Holy Spirit but the people refused to accept their need of Him. The previous pastor taught against such things. But now God has done it. Thanks for making yourself available,' he told me.

Jan was still suffering almost permanently with a bad stomach. The food didn't suit her. She went to lie down and I heard her singing praises as I walked past the room. Two hours later, she emerged.

'I was so fed up. I hated the thought that I might have to go back to England early. I decided to praise God and sing until I was healed. And now all the pain has gone and I believe God has healed me permanently.'

'Praise God!' I said, giving her a hug.

Our mission in Kenya was over. Next stop was Uganda. We sat in the small departure lounge of Wilson Airport, waiting for the flight with MAF (Mission Aviation Fellowship). A smartly dressed Kenyan lady came into the room with a clipboard in her hand. 'Miss Parsons?' she inquired. 'You're travelling with Miss Jan Marchant, aren't you?'

'Yes,' I replied.

'Your luggage is overweight. You'll have to leave something behind. Wait there a minute. I'll come back and let you know how many kilos you have to remove.'

'What was that about?' Jan asked.

I explained the situation to her. 'I suppose we'll have to leave the bag with all the pastors' teaching cassettes and books. It weighs about twenty kilos,' I mused, pausing to think for a moment. 'But if God used us to bring that material all the way from England to bless pastors, and we managed to get it into Kenya, there's no way we should have to abandon it here.' Jesus said, "Whatever two of you on earth agree, it will be done by my Father in heaven." So what do you reckon, Jan? Let's agree that all our luggage gets on this flight.'

'Definitely,' she replied. We shook hands and said, 'Thank You, Father, for the miracle.'

The lady returned. 'We've asked someone else to leave his luggage behind,' she said. 'He's got many bags so we chose him instead of you.' She walked away and Jan and I cheered quietly, so as not to disturb anyone in the lounge.

7

One Sows and Another Reaps

Most things worth doing are accompanied by pain

Why was it that, at Entebbe Airport, there was never anyone to meet me? I had written to inform Richard and Justine Bakadde of our arrival, but maybe the post had been too slow. We really couldn't justify spending £15 on a private taxi into Kampala. I tried to phone Richard's office but after an hour I gave up as I was not getting through. We met Tom, a MAF technician in the airport. He was on his way to the city and gave us a free lift in his pick-up.

'Oh look, there's a sign saying 'zebra crossing'. Do you think zebras come into the city?' asked Jan absent-mindedly. As soon as the words left her mouth she realised what she'd said. The Rift Valley had certainly made an impact.

Reaching the Bakaddes' office, I ran up the stairs to find them. I turned the corner, only to find that all the walls had been knocked down and there was rubble on the floor. The whole place was being renovated. I asked the men working on the building, 'Has Business Care Promotions moved?' But they didn't understand English. I skipped down the stairs and looked along the corridor.

'Hello, can I help you?' a lady called out from her desk.

'Oh yes, please. Do you know where these upstairs offices have moved?'

'No, sorry,' she replied.

We tried telephoning again, but it was hopeless. The line wouldn't connect. Although Tom had just finished a night shift, he drove us to Miracle Centre. We met some pastors who directed us to an open-air crusade in town where we could find Harriet. We stopped by the roadside, where someone recognised me and greeted me with great enthusiasm. I couldn't remember who he was, but he went to fetch Harriet. She came bounding towards us, looking really well, her face radiating the light of Jesus and her hair newly styled with 'extensions', the artificial plaits which are added to the hair. She hugged me tightly and did a little dance, squealing with delight because I had come.

We went together to Robert Kayanja's new house.

'There's plenty of room, so you can stay with us,' Harriet said.

'Well, we're supposed to be staying with Justine and Richard,' I told her.

We drove through the main street of town, the pavements a mass of heaving humanity. At the same moment Harriet and I saw Richard Bakadde walking amongst the crowd. 'Stop!' we shouted to Tom, who pulled over swiftly. We jumped out of the pick-up and rushed towards Richard before he could disappear. He was surprised to see me and had obviously not heard I was coming.

'I'm here with my friend Jan. We'll come and see you some time,' I said.

Harriet was delighted we could stay with her for a few days before she left for England. She had been accepted to spend two terms at Roffey Place and the Lord had miraculously provided the money for her ticket.

Later, we joined Justine and Richard in their lovely big house. They gave up their large bedroom so we could enjoy the double bed and the view from the balcony. Christmas Day came and went. I didn't miss the commercialism of the West, but I was surprised to find that I missed some of the English trimmings.

A few days after Christmas a friend of ours from Horsham came to visit for three weeks. Sam Rohloff, whom I describe as a teenage pensioner, could cycle an average of two hundred miles per week. He would get up to pray at 5.00 most mornings and carried the joy of the Lord throughout the day. He was a tremendous blessing to have around. He caused a great stir in the taxi park as people shouted, '*Muzungu Mzee!*' (*Mzee* is a term of respect used for an elderly person.) His grey hair and also his laugh turned heads in public.

We all accompanied Richard, Justine and Johnson to a fellowship barbecue at the house of the previous vice-president of Uganda. He had invited many government ministers and church leaders to come together and pray for the new year, declaring God's righteousness over the country. It was a powerful time, and many no-compromise messages were given. The television cameras were there and we were an obvious attraction, being white.

Justine dressed Jan and me in the traditional Ugandan costume for women, termed a *busuti* or a *gomesi*. These long silky dresses are worn right to the ground with a sash tied around the middle and hanging down with tassels at the bottom. The short puffy sleeves give it a distinctive style. Jan and I travelled in the back of an open pick-up, and many screams could be heard along the road as people saw the strange sight of a *muzungu* in a *gomesi*.

For the new year, we had a retreat in a peaceful place by the edge of Lake Victoria. A Bible teacher called Laban Jjumba taught us from morning to night in a relaxed, easy-to-follow manner. The points he brought out were interesting and God was speaking. We fasted throughout the three days and spent time waiting on the Lord. I received a new anointing of joy. It was so refreshing to receive after giving in Kenya. We prayed the new year in. At midnight, we found a partner to prophesy to, which was very powerful, and we basked in the Lord's love and goodness for several hours.

After the retreat we visited people I knew from my previous trip. We also attended some Miracle Centre meetings. One time, Sam was called up on to the stage and Robert Kayanja prophesied: 'God is going to take you into many nations and He will use you for His purposes. He is restoring your youth like the eagle.' This opened wide the doors of possibility for Sam. God subsequently sent him to different nations.

Sometimes, Richard and Justine would wake their children up to pray in the early hours of the morning. Sam was always willing to get up for prayer. Richard shared from the Bible and Sam dozed off to sleep, emerging with a loud, 'Amen!' at quite an inappropriate place, much to the amusement of everyone. Sam told me that once, in England, he fell asleep while reading a passage of scripture aloud in church. He's the only person I've known who can drift off in mid-sentence or fall asleep with a forkful of food in his mouth!

We enjoyed our time in Uganda. It was encouraging to be in a country where the supernatural was a normal part of life in Christ.

'I think God's purpose was to refresh us before we move on,' I said.

'He has done something wonderful for me. I feel so liberated inside,' Jan told me. 'This month has been one of the most worthwhile times of my life.'

Our next destination was Zimbabwe. We booked a flight with Zambia Airways and flew to Harare. We stayed for a few nights in a hotel to pray and get rested and 'unpeopled'. Walking around the centre of Harare, Jan and I could not believe our eyes. 'It's so clean,' said Jan, thinking back to the dusty, orange streets of Kampala. 'And look at those huge buildings.'

'I can't get over these clean glass windows in the shops, and there's so much available. They probably import a lot of stuff from South Africa,' I added thoughtfully. 'This city could be anywhere in Europe.'

Restaurants and shops lined the wide streets of Harare. 'They built the roads wide enough to turn a horse and cart,' we were told. Jan and I enjoyed walking the streets, admiring everything. It was a shock to see so many white people in the city, after being in places where there were so few or even none at all.

While walking back from having a much-needed hair cut, we kept being plagued by a young man. He was drunk and we tried to lose him, turning corners fast and hiding under the umbrellas outside the Wimpy. But I soon realised God wanted me to witness to his aching, desperate heart. While I spoke, a heaviness came over him and a demon manifested. We took authority in the name of Jesus. Then he prayed the sinner's prayer. Jan and I laid hands on him sitting there in public, and God ministered to him.

'Phew!' he said, 'that was powerful. And you know what? I don't even feel drunk any more. Many of my friends are into drugs and booze. I don't know what they'll say when they hear I've turned religious.'

We encouraged him, opening the Bible to show him different scriptures. 'If you carry on living for Jesus, those people will see such a change in your life that they'll want to know what's happened. Many will come to know the Lord through you,' we told him.

On the Sunday we went with him to a Pentecostal church. The presence of God could be felt but the way they conducted the service was very traditional.

'I don't think I can fit in with these people,' he told us, and he seemed relieved when we agreed.

'What you need is a church where they see the same things happening as in the Bible, where Jesus is working miracles and touching people's lives. You need to meet people who really know Him personally and involve Him in every part of their lives. We'll keep looking for a church for you and we'll be in touch.'

He gave us his telephone number and reluctantly said goodbye. We later put him in touch with Pastor Hezekiah, whose church was some distance away from where he lived. Jan had said, 'Next time we meet you you'll probably be married with two children.' He wrote to us in England telling us that in fact he was already married and had two children whom he had not told us about.

Jan and I lay on our hotel beds, resting one afternoon. 'Jan, look. There's a telephone directory in this place,' I said, surprised. 'Let's see if we can find Hezekiah's number.' He was the next pastor we were due to visit.

'Here's Apostolic Faith Church,' I said, looking down the list, 'and Apostolic Faith Mission. Wow, there are so many churches with similar names, and we don't even know the exact name of his church.'

'We'll just have to try different ones,' said Jan.

'Yes, but let's wait until we're thoroughly rested before we phone, because once they know we're here, we'll be busy preaching non-stop again,' I told her.

When we finally phoned we tried several numbers before finding the right one.

'Yes, I did get your letter,' said Hezekiah. 'Where are you now?'

'We're in Harare,' I told him.

'Where? At the airport?'

'No, we're staying in a hotel.'

He agreed to come and pick us up in a borrowed vehicle. Soon the receptionist phoned our room: 'Pastor Hezekiah is here to see you.'

'Beautiful! Beautiful!' he said, smiling at us both, as we came down the stairs.

At his house, Hezekiah introduced us to his wife and children. His church was one of forty-two of that denomination in the Harare area. Jan and I sat in the evening meeting, watching the proceedings. It was hard not to make comparisons with Uganda which was still fresh in our minds. 'God has blessed us with two new daughters,' Hezekiah told the congregation, 'and they have come fully grown.' The people laughed.

We were given names in Shona, a language of Zimbabwe, as ours were completely unpronounceable to the local people. I was called Nyasha, which means grace, and Jan was Ngoni, meaning mercy. We soon learnt to answer to our names whenever we were called. We were also taught how to greet in Shona. The ladies cup their hands in rhythm with the words, bowing slightly. The men do a similar thing, clapping with straight hands.

Jan and I slept in a double bed which had been evacuated by one of Hezekiah and Prisca's sons. The first night I hardly slept. It was very hot and the blue plastic mattress cover crackled every time one of us moved. I lay still, resting in the Lord's presence, His love burning in my heart. 'I've been praying almost the whole night,' I told Jan.

'I've prayed in tongues a lot since coming here. It seems God's about to do something,' she said.

Soon we were given an opportunity to preach to the students, staff and church members at the Bible College just outside the city. There was a battle inside me against fear, but Jan and I prayed together in the small reception area before going into the main hall. 'Lord, just do Your work,' I pleaded, tears streaming down my face.

I felt completely inadequate to be speaking in such an establishment but I moved my focus away from myself and on to the One who lives in me. We broke through into victory. I remembered Colin telling me once, before we were to minister in a leaders' meeting, 'It's not your qualifications or experience that enable God to use you. It's your relationship with Jesus that allows Him to flow through. Just stay close to Him and listen to Him.'

I sat in the front and enjoyed the praise and worship time, still not knowing what I should speak on. 'Just share what's on your heart,' I heard the Holy Spirit say. I stood up and brought a message from Luke 9 about taking up the cross. I told the story of the transfiguration, where the disciples experienced the glory of God and came down the mountain to face the challenges of ministry. I spoke about the Great Commission to go and preach the gospel. The people were with me one hundred per cent, even though my preaching technique was far from professional. The Holy Spirit was so obviously present and people dedicated themselves afresh to God. As they did so, many experienced His glory. Their faces shone as they did 'heart-business' with Him.

The Lord gave me some words of knowledge and ministered to sorrowful hearts. It was a precious time in the love of God. After the meeting, my interpreter came up to me. 'Thanks for interpreting,' I said. 'You're so good I hardly noticed you were there.'

He looked at me with tears in his eyes. 'What you preached has really touched my heart,' he told me. 'I've been fasting for the last nine days because of exactly what you've been saying. I have such a desire to see God moving.'

That night, I couldn't get to sleep. It seemed that God was doing a reviving work in my heart. I got up to pray and gave God an opportunity to speak. The following day Jan preached in a ladies' meeting about relationship with the Holy Spirit. We prayed together with the ladies and Jesus baptised them in His Holy Spirit.

One morning, we taught the students at the Bible College. I spoke about being dead, buried and resurrected with Christ. It was encouraging to see revelation hitting people, but a few didn't grasp the fact that it should be applied to one's life by faith, and I had little time to explain further. Jan's session was excellent. She talked about the power of the spoken Word of God and how to pray using the scripture.

In the afternoon there was another meeting. The Lord

gave me words of knowledge for earache. Three people came forward and were visibly touched by God's power. Shock waves went through the college and I wondered if they were used to seeing God at work in such a way.

We continued to minister in the Bible College and in churches. Each afternoon, we had supper at different church members' homes, eating between 4.30 p.m. and 5.00 p.m. The timing suited me better than the Ugandan midnight meals.

One of the most significant visits was with a man called Wireless, an elder of Hezekiah's church. After supper we prayed with some of his family. Jan and I laid hands on Wireless and prophesied. The revelation started flowing.

'Do you have pain in your toes?' I asked. He nodded, his head still down in prayer. We prayed for him and God removed the pain.

'Does your eldest son have intestinal problems?' I asked. They confirmed that it was true and someone went to find him. While he was coming, Jan started speaking, 'I believe God is healing someone's eye,' she said, looking around at the people. We prayed for that person and Jan continued. 'The Lord is going to provide the wood you need for your house,' she said boldly, not knowing in the natural that the roof had not yet been completed. We laid hands on the young man with the problem in the intestines and another son came in. The Holy Spirit showed me that his neck needed healing, so we prayed for him too. 'And the Lord promises to provide for your daughter's school fees,' I prophesied. We were so excited by what God was doing for this family. We left the house full of laughter and praise for our wonderful God who cares so much about every detail. It was an evening that none of us would forget.

We met their son a couple of days later. 'I'm completely

healed now,' he told us. 'God is so great. He didn't just heal me, but something else happened. I wasn't really interested in church or God, but He's done something in my heart. I've changed and I'll never be the same again.'

'Glory to God!' Jan and I rejoiced, enthusiastically.

After two weeks, it was time to move on. We telephoned Bulawayo, a town in the south-west of Zimbabwe where a lovely little lady called Grace lived. She was a white Zimbabwean who had come to Roffey Place as a mature student.

'Some friends of yours are here in Bulawayo,' she told us over the phone.

'Who's that then?' I inquired.

'Jim and Megan Prestige,' she answered. 'They say they met you in Israel on your trip with Kingdom Faith.'

My mind went back to the middle-aged couple who Jan and I had got on so well with.

'We're going to live in Africa,' they had told me.

'See you there!' I had joked, knowing how unlikely it would be in such a large continent.

'They've invited you and Jan to visit a game park with them,' Grace continued. 'They're working at a teacher training college and need to travel. There's room in the back of their van, if you don't mind travelling a bit rough, and they'll pay for your stay at the game park for a couple of nights.'

Jan's eyes lit up when she heard of the wonderful opportunity. 'It's just God!' she said.

'Yes,' I agreed, 'Isn't the timing perfect? They're leaving the day after we arrive in Bulawayo.'

Hezekiah drove us to the airport. 'We're coming back on Saturday,' I assured Prisca, noticing her sad face.

'See you soon!' said Jan, waving happily.

Grace had a lovely house which seemed luxurious to

Jan and me after months of travelling. We dived in her small garden swimming-pool and enjoyed the peace and quiet. The next day Jim and Megan picked us up and we set off for Hwange National Park. Jan and I slept for most of the journey but towards the end we saw many elephants from the road, and giraffes straining their tall necks to eat leaves on the tree-tops. We stopped at various look-out points. Once we saw an elephant having fun in a pool of water. I borrowed Jim's binoculars and placed my camera behind the lens.

'What are you doing?' they asked.

'Just trying something out,' I answered, taking a photo through the binoculars. It came out quite nicely.

At the lodge, the view from our apartment was magnificent. I thought of the scripture I had read so many times: 'Your eyes will view a land which stretches afar.' I wondered how many miles I could see as I gazed across the tops of the green trees stretching away into the distance.

'It's a bit like my life really,' I said to Jan, philosophically. 'You never quite know what's beyond the horizon. God is full of surprises. Before God spoke to me, I had never imagined I would come to Africa.'

We slept solidly that night and lazed about most of the next day and unwound, which was exactly what we both needed. 'It feels strange not to be preaching,' we told Megan and Jim.

'Well, we feel it's a bit like Elijah who slept and ate and then ran in the strength of that,' Megan said, showing us the verses in the Bible.

At 4.00 p.m. we went for a walk down an elephant track with a guide.

'I don't carry this rifle because of the animals,' he told us. 'It's the poachers you need to watch out for. One of our workers was shot dead a few weeks ago by a poacher from Zambia. So if I see him first, I'll shoot him before he shoots me. I've never used a gun on an animal in twenty years of working here,' he said.

We walked for two hours and came within six metres of a large elephant. It didn't see us. 'These old elephants often go away from the rest of the group,' he whispered as we hid ourselves behind the leaves of a bush. Later, he pointed out different tracks in the mud. 'That's the marking of a hyena,' he said, 'and that one must be a rhino.'

'What about this one?' I asked.

'That's the footprint of a buffalo,' he told us. 'You wouldn't want to meet one down here,' he said, pulling a face. 'You'd have to climb a tree, if possible.'

'What about the lions?' I asked. 'Are they dangerous?'

'Not around here,' he told us. 'There's plenty of game for them to eat.'

Next morning, I was glad to remember his words when we were greeted by the roar of a lion down in the valley. We left early, as Jim and Megan had to visit eight schools in the area to see how their students were doing with their teaching practice. Two minutes into our journey, Megan whispered, 'Slow down, Jim. Ssshhh!'

Jan and I looked out of the window. There across the track was a pride of lions. '. . . nine, ten, eleven,' we counted.

They sat calmly on either side of the road and two of them shifted as we drove slowly towards them, stopping to take photos. I wound down the window an inch and took a close-up of a very contented, friendly-looking lioness, swishing her tail without a concern in the world, her eyes closed like a cat enjoying a good stroke.

We drove off slowly. 'Thank You, Jesus!' we shouted when we were a safe distance away.

'I prayed we would see some lions,' Megan told us.

'So did I,' said Jan.

'God is good,' we all agreed.

Jim and Megan dropped us off at a junction and went on their way. Jan and I were believing God for a lift to Victoria Falls. After only five minutes, a van passed us and then slowed down, reversing back to where we were. A young African man opened the door. 'Jump in,' he said.

As we came closer to the van, I noticed the Christian stickers in the windows. Looking at the four young men, I asked them, 'Are you born again?'

'Yes,' they told me. 'What about you?'

'Yes, we are,' I answered. 'Actually, we're missionaries, although it doesn't look much like it when we wear these shorts. We've just finished four months of ministry and we're in tourist mode for a few days,' I said, smiling.

'We're holding a crusade near Victoria Falls,' one of them said. 'That's what all this equipment is for. Actually, the reason we stopped for you was so we could tell you about the Lord.'

We enjoyed sharing with those young men on the journey. We could see they were in close relationship with Jesus. One of them told us a true story:

'We have some friends who went to preach in a remote village. While they were walking to the place, they were shocked to find themselves face to face with a buffalo which started to charge. One man managed to jump up a tree and watched as his friend ran and fell in a narrow ditch. Once a buffalo catches up with you, he can trample you to death. This buffalo kept trampling, but somehow its hooves missed the man's body. But the soil covered him as the buffalo cavorted around. He started to suffocate, so his only option was to get up, asking God what to do. He found himself holding on to the buffalo's horns, staring into the face of the creature, eye to eye, only inches away. The Lord gave him supernatural strength and ability. After several minutes, he let go of the horns and the buffalo ran away, scared. The two men proceeded to the crusade meeting, They told the people what had just happened. Many were saved as a result.'

After some good fellowship, we left the young men, our hearts full. The Victoria Falls were great, but there was not much water due to the recent drought in Zimbabwe and Zambia. While we were there, it poured with rain. We tried to shelter under a rock, unsuccessfully. We walked to a hotel drenched through, and sat on the comfortable chairs and drank a hot cup of tea, deciding what to do next. We visited a nearby crocodile farm as that was the cheapest option. The jaws of the crocodile snapped at a large joint of meat thrown down to it. I rather liked the baby crocs and even held one which was five weeks old and the size of a small lizard.

We caught a steam train which travelled through the night to Bulawayo. The cabin had bunk beds with leather covers and the walls were made from beautiful wood. We opened the window and lay down, enjoying a good night until we reached Bulawayo the next morning.

In Bulawayo we were disappointed to find that the money we'd been promised had not yet been transferred from England to the bank. So we cancelled our flight back to Harare and waited. We couldn't contact Hezekiah and Prisca to let them know of our arrangements because the telephone lines were out of order. We checked the bank in town several times, to no avail.

'No worries. God is in control,' I said.

The fact that we were stranded didn't seem so bad in the light of how God worked that week as we ministered in schools, house fellowships and church meetings. 'We haven't experienced such a move of God for years!' an elderly couple testified, after one meeting.

'I think I know what Jesus meant, when He said He felt the power going out of him,' I told Jan. 'I feel completely drained after that session.'

'Yeah, let's spend time with the Lord, receiving from Him,' she suggested.

We had a lovely time in God's presence, communing with the Holy Spirit and sharing what we felt He was saying to us.

Every day, we checked at the bank for our money. A manager really sympathised with us when he heard we were stuck in Bulawayo and were due to fly to Zambia. He took it upon himself to trace the money, and after a week it was in our possession, having passed through four different banks.

We said goodbye to dear Grace, flew back to Harare and stayed with Hezekiah and Prisca for two nights. I preached once again at the Bible College and we were lavished with gifts: chair-back covers and machine-knitted jumpers among other things. I will never forget seeing the young students rushing towards us as we pulled away in the canvas-covered pick-up. One girl thrust a newspaper parcel into my hands. 'I'm sorry I couldn't wash it first,' she told me. When I unwrapped it, I recognised the pretty embroidered blouse she had worn in the church. Jan and I were blessed by their giving hearts. It really touched us to see the students giving their best out of their poverty. They were giving to God and we knew He would give back to them a good measure. The clothes were useful to us because the few outfits we had were fading in the sun and rapidly wearing out through constant hand-washing.

From Harare we sent a telegram to Bupe Latima, the ex-Roffey student who lived in the north of Zambia. He was working with Ambassadors for Christ, headed by Timothy Chilufya who had also been a student at Roffey Place. He had sent Bupe there for some training. We wanted to see both of these men if possible, but heard that Timothy was out of the country.

In Bulawayo some of the white Africans told us, 'Oh, you're going to Zambia. There's so much disease and poverty there. We'll be praying for your protection. They've been hit harder than us by the recent drought and it's a very poor country. I should take some provisions if I were you.' We bought some milk powder and a few other preserved foods, but refused to be discouraged by those reports.

'God will look after us, and I'm sure it's not as bad as they say. We'll see how we find it,' I said to Jan.

8

The Harvest is Plentiful . . .

Don't see yourself as anything; see God as everything

In Lusaka, the capital of Zambia, we stayed with a friend
of Hezekiah's. Some young men carried several sponge
mattresses upstairs, piling up seven of them on the floor
to form beds for us.

'I think I'll just use one,' I said, pressing my hand on
the pile of mattresses, imagining an avalanche in the night.

The Zambian people seemed very friendly. We had a
meal with some German missionaries and prayed together.
The Lord revealed to Jan some of the difficulties they

were facing in their church and God used us to encourage and comfort them. It was a very fruitful evening. That night, I had such a desire to pray. In a supernatural way, God planted a love in my heart for Zambia and I knew this would not be my last time in the country. President Chiluba, a born-again Christian, had declared Zambia a Christian nation, and the peace I experienced was evidence enough.

Early in the morning, we flew to a small town called Mansa, which had a simple airstrip. We carried our suitcases in the heat across the mud runway towards a small building. From there we were taken by pick-up to the town centre.

'How do we get to Kawambwa?' I asked the driver, but he didn't understand what I was saying. He dropped us off and drove away, leaving us standing with our heavy bags around us. Someone directed us to the bus station and we sat by the roadside and waited.

The handle of my suitcase had broken and as there was a shoe mender's in that area, we took it for repair. A little man sewed it with a thread and a sharp needle while we perched on Jan's bag in the shade of a hot corrugated iron building. 'It's not good, it's not good,' the little man said, looking around nervously. After a few inquiries we realised he was warning us that the area was known for thieves and thugs and there were several demon-possessed people walking around. We were a target, two white girls surrounded by luggage, but there was nowhere else to wait for the bus. So we remained at the roadside, trusting God for His divine protection. I found my Bible and we read a chapter each out loud, taking turns while the other listened. Five long hours went by. We were pleased we had brought some bread rolls, bananas and bottled water with us.

At last, the post bus rattled its way into the town, puffing black exhaust into the faces of people walking by the roadside. It stopped and people pushed and shoved to get on. Jan and I had the same thought. 'How are we going to get on with all our luggage?'

A young man saw our dilemma and raced to the entrance of the bus, forcing his way up the steps and shouting about the *bazungu*. Reluctantly, people made way for us and our luggage was thrown up on top of the bus and tied down with bits of rope. We found two seats covered with broken plastic and sat down, sweating. 'Praise God!' we sighed, trying to maintain our peace in the midst of the shouting and chaos. Jan was praying in tongues under her breath.

A man got on the bus and staggered up the aisle. His matted hair and his open brown shirt, originally white, indicated he was either drunk or mad. As he reached us, he pointed at Jan and me dramatically.

'What are you doing here? Have you come to preach the Word of God?' he said in a mocking tone of voice. The eyes of everybody were on us. Someone grabbed the man and shoved him on to a seat.

'Demons, I expect,' I whispered to Jan. 'Thank You, Lord, for Your protection,' we prayed quietly.

The post bus pulled away and after a while we made conversation with a young businessman from Zaïre. He spoke French and was pleased to discover that we understood, although Jan knew a lot more of the language than I did. Within minutes, Jan was explaining the gospel to the young man who translated it loudly into Bemba, one of the Zambian languages. People as far as four rows in front of us strained their ears to hear.

Jan led our interpreter and his Tanzanian friend in a prayer. They declared, 'The devil no longer has authority

over me; I renounce all works of darkness from my life.'
The bus suddenly swerved to the right and the left.
Another bus hurtled towards us at top speed, just missing
the window where we were sitting. The driver managed to
gain control and all the passengers murmured, while Jan
and the two young men continued in prayer with their
heads bowed. The bus stopped and people shouted to the
driver in Bemba. Then three men ran to the back, grabbed
the mad man and forced him out of the bus, flinging him
into a ditch. We were far from any town or village. The
bus drove off again. 'Maybe they thought that man was
causing the problem, bringing us bad luck or something,'
Jan and I speculated.

We continued on our long journey, stopping at every
village post office to drop off letters and parcels. At each
place there was a great commotion as people scuffled
about on the roof and passengers shouted. The young man
who had helped us on the bus explained. 'People are so
poor here, they are trying to steal the luggage on top. I'll
keep checking your cases for you.' He pushed his way
past the panicking passengers and jumped off the bus,
returning a few moments later.

'Yes, your bags are still there,' he told us.

'I suppose we take his word for it,' I said to Jan. The
only alternative was to get mobbed in the frantic crowd
surrounding the bus. Once again we prayed, placing our
lives and our possessions in God's hands.

One time, when the bus pulled away, everyone shouted
to the driver and the bus came to a halt. Someone was
still on the roof, trying to throw a bag down to his friend
below. The conductor threatened the thief as he climbed
down the iron ladder at the back of the bus. We set off
again.

Sometimes when we stopped, people at the side of the

road rushed over to sell their bananas, oranges and pieces of goat meat and beef on sticks, stretching their wares up towards the bus windows. There was a flurry of hands, as screwed-up *kwacha* notes (the Zambian currency) and food were passed from person to person in a rushed attempt to do business before the bus jogged to a start and smoked its way onwards.

'I think I'll call this "pothole express",' I said to Jan, laughing, as the bus banged over the deep ruts in the road. We travelled for hours and it was dark by the time we reached the small town of Kazembe. Jan and I sat on our seat until most of the people had alighted. A short young man, dressed in a blue suit, peered anxiously in the windows. His face lit up when he saw us.

'Glory to God!' he said in a low, husky voice, and rushed over to shake our hands, laughing infectiously. 'I'm Mark Kaoma and I work with Bupe. Praise God you've arrived safely. We had people stationed in different places waiting for you, and we only received your telegram yesterday. Bupe is looking forward to seeing you, but we may have to sleep in Kazembe because there's no transport to Kawambwa at this time of night.'

I was in a daze and didn't really mind at that point what happened. It was good to meet someone so obviously full of the Spirit of God. We knew we were in safe hands. Within minutes, God worked a miracle for us. We met a lorry driver going to Kawambwa that evening. Mark negotiated a good price and we travelled for two hours in the pitch black, relaxing in the cabin of the lorry, silently praying. The driver took us through the town of Kawambwa and into Kawambwa Boys' Secondary School.

A slender, intelligent-looking man ran out of his house. It was Bupe. What a welcome we received. He obviously knew what it meant to make such a journey. He introduced us to his smiling wife, Vera, who didn't speak much English. We said hello to his seven children and prayed together. They placed some food on the table and everyone left the lounge. Jan and I sat waiting for them to come back, but after a while we realised they must be eating somewhere else. We learnt that this was the custom in Zambia: new visitors always eat alone.

We walked in the dark to a well-built brick house where two teachers called Abraham and Webber lived, and we were shown to a room with a double mattress on the floor, placed there especially for us. Bupe took me aside.

'Is this room OK for you?' he asked, a concerned expression on his face.

'This is great. Don't you worry. We're adapting ourselves to every situation, and believe me, this is luxury compared to some places I've stayed,' I told him. We had running water and a flushing toilet, electricity, mosquito netting at the windows, and it was a quiet place. What more could one ask for?

I woke up in the morning wondering where I was, and saw Jan sleeping next to me. I sat up and prayed and read my Bible. The weather was quite cool, as that area was high and there had been some rain. I went outside to look around. This was the greenest place we had seen for a while. Two columns of tall eucalyptus trees lined the road to the school, forming an avenue. I wondered who had planted them and how long they had been there.

I met Bupe walking from his house. He taught me how to greet in Bemba. '*Mulishani?*' he asked. 'That means "how are you?" Now you answer, "*bwino*".'

'What does *bwino* mean?'

'It means "I'm fine".'

'But what if you're not fine?' I queried.

'Well, we always say we're fine and then maybe in the

course of the conversation we might say what's really happening,' he explained. 'By the way, I'm arranging a programme for you to preach in schools and different churches. The headmaster here has agreed to let you minister to the whole school today, which is a wonderful opportunity. I've drafted up a schedule for one week. How long will you be able to stay?' he asked.

'There's no real time limit. Two or three weeks?' I suggested. Bupe was pleased; they really wanted to make use of us.

Back at the house I found Jan kneeling down praying, her head covered over with a *gitenge*. She looked up and I saw pink marks on her forehead where her fingers had been pressed against the skin.

'You've got "prayer marks"!' I teased.

Jan was always ready for a good laugh and retaliated with a witty comment.

We ate a plate of pumpkin for breakfast and Bupe prayed a quick prayer before we left, as was his habit. It was good to acknowledge God at intervals throughout the day. Bupe took us around to meet different staff in the school. It would have been an offence not to have done so, but I was still feeling rather weary from the journey and was somewhat anxious to spend time in prayer before preaching to the pupils.

The school gathered outside one of the classrooms and I stood on the balcony with Mark, who interpreted. It was a struggle to start with, but the Holy Spirit came through. Jan was praying silently in the front row. 'Go for it, girl!' her facial expression seemed to say.

'You are either a slave to righteousness or a slave to sin,' I told the boys. 'There's no in between and the choice is yours.' The crowd fell into thoughtful silence as I spoke and the Holy Spirit did His convicting work. At the end somewhere between thirty and forty boys made a courageous step, walking forward in front of their peers to respond to God. Such joy filled my heart.

On Sunday, we had the pleasure of baptising ten boys in the stream. The Christian Union in the school was strong and Bupe was always on hand, so we knew our work had been worthwhile.

On Monday we had a free day and went to Kawambwa in the pouring rain. The town was about forty minutes' walk from the school and consisted of a bank, a post office and a petrol station which was infrequently supplied with fuel. There was a shop run by Indians, a small cafe, a couple of bars, various small shops, a market-place and a few houses.

I went to observe the condition of the runway further out of town. I ran along the orange gravel airstrip, my hands in the air, singing at the top of my voice, 'The Lord reigns, let the earth rejoice!' On my way back, I asked a woman, 'Do planes ever land here?'

She went to ask her friend. 'Yes,' her friend said.

'How often do they come?' I asked. I could see them thinking but they seemed unsure. 'About once a month?' I suggested.

'No. Maybe once a year or once in two years,' they told me.

From town we visited a Christian teacher in a girls' school in Kawambwa. Otti was from Ghana and I recognised the same fire and zeal in him as I had seen in the Nigerian Christians.

'I'm completely behind you on this mission,' he told us. 'I'm praying and fasting for all your efforts to be multiplied in bringing souls into the Kingdom of God in this area. You're going to see God doing mighty things beyond your expectations,' he encouraged. 'I wanted to arrange for you to minister here at this school, but the headmistress recently beat some girls for casting out demons and isn't co-operative at present. But I'll talk to her again,' he promised.

We went to a beautiful place called Ntumbacushi Falls where a stream winds its way around the rocky terrain, cascading into a large waterfall with several smaller ones further downstream. We found a pool where we could swim.

'Hey, what's that?' said Jan suddenly, pointing to the nearby vegetation.

'Monkeys,' said Bupe, and we watched as they scuttled away nervously.

The water was cold because of the previous rainfall. Bupe and Abraham dived off the rocks while Jan and I swam gracefully round the natural pool. The current was really strong. I sat on a rock and let go, allowing myself be carried along in the shallow water to the next cluster of rocks. I did this several times, which was great fun. But at one point I lost control and went sweeping down a fast-flowing channel. Once I realised what was happening, I turned over on to my front, feeling for something to hold on to. I dug my knees into the rough rock below to slow myself down, scraping them as the current pushed me along.

Jan was standing on the bank and caught sight of me. Our eyes met and I saw an anxious look on her face. It was as if time stood still. Even then, I trusted that God would intervene. My hands felt the slippery rock below me and to my relief I found a small hole where I managed to lodge two of my fingers while the rest of my body was buffeted by the water at arm's length. Abraham rushed towards me and I wondered how long I could hold on. It seemed like an eternity before he was beside me reaching out his hand and grabbing my free arm, yanking me up to safety. Just nine metres away down the fast-flowing stream was a rocky three-metre fall.

I sat on the rock getting my breath back and Jan came beside me. After I had recovered she told her account of the story. 'I saw a flash of pink swimming costume and couldn't believe you were heading towards that waterfall.' We thanked God for His protection.

The following day, we went to a Presbyterian church. 'These people are not true believers; they're just religious,' Bupe told us. 'In fact it's only because you're English that they're allowing you to preach. I could never preach here, but I'll interpret for you.'

When I began to speak, there was a disturbance at the back of the church. Five large women fled from the building as fast as their legs could take them. I kept speaking, unmoved by what was happening. We were in spiritual warfare but nothing could stop the Word going out, and it would certainly accomplish what it was sent to do.

I preached about Nicodemus going to Jesus in secret, emphasising the point Jesus made that we must be born again if we are to see the Kingdom of God. I explained what it meant. At the end, the whole church, as many as forty people, jumped to their feet with their arms raised. They walked to the front. Even the church secretary, who had been there for years, humbled himself and came out of his seat. Jan and I laid hands on each individual and prayed, delighted at what God had done.

Afterwards we spoke to the Spirit-filled pastor and his wife. They had been posted to the remote town of Kawambwa only two months ago, where it was hoped they would not cause such a disturbance with their radical faith in that traditional denomination.

'There's your work for you,' I told the pastor. 'Now

you can disciple and teach them. They're in your hands.'

The Lord had been waking me up to pray for two hours each night. We were certainly gaining territory for Jesus and the devil didn't like it. Sometimes it seemed so hard to pray and break through into the Lord's presence, not because I'd done anything wrong but because of the environment we were in. There was a lot of witchcraft in that area. Although Bupe and Mark didn't say much, I realised that they spent a lot of time praying for our protection and that God would move.

We preached in the tea estate some distance away, having searched for petrol for a couple of hours as there was none in the petrol station. We paid an extortionate price to someone who had stored some. I also drove to a girls' school in another town. The pastor was unprepared to receive us. The written message confirming our coming had been thrown through the kitchen window and landed in a bucket of water. However, we preached and thirty-two girls came to the Lord, demons left and the Christians were encouraged. It was too far to return that night so Jan and I shared a single mattress.

'Hey Jan, listen to this. ' "Lord, you establish peace for us; all that we have accomplished you have done for us." ' Isn't that a great verse?'

'Mmm,' she said meditating on the words before drifting off to sleep.

We arrived back in Kawambwa to find that yet another person had died in the locality. That was the seventh person in two weeks. 'We're going to the funeral,' Bupe told us. 'Would you like to come?'

I glanced at Jan to see what she was thinking and she didn't look too keen.

'I don't think so. We'd appreciate staying here for a rest,' I told Bupe.

'It wouldn't be like an English funeral. You could preach. Many are saved at African burials,' he said.

'That's great, but I think we'll stay back this time,' I responded. We saved our energy for the next mission.

Jan and I enjoyed the seven-kilometre walk to Kazembe. I saw a lady walking with bare feet, carrying a baby on her back and a load on her head.

'Why have I got shoes and she hasn't?' I asked myself. I felt like taking them off and giving them to her but I thought my feet wouldn't survive the journey on that stony track.

On arrival we went into the pastor's lovely mud house and sat in their small lounge. A mountain of *nshima* was placed on the wooden table with dishes of tiny silver fish called *chisense*, served in a tomato sauce.

'This is our staple food,' the pastor said, pointing to the steaming cornflour cake. 'If you don't eat *nshima* you haven't eaten food.'

A lady brought a jug of water, some soap and a bowl for us to wash our hands. 'This is nice,' said Jan as the lady poured warm water over her hands, holding the plastic bowl underneath.

In turn everyone took a chunk of hot *nshima* with their hands and placed it in their dishes. I copied what they did.

'Ouch! It's hot!' I said, quickly removing my hand.

The others tried to conceal their amusement. Mark took hold of my hand to see how soft the skin was and offered to serve Jan and me.

After we had prayed I discreetly watched to see how they would eat the food. They took a small piece of *nshima* and rolled it in their fingers. Then they dipped it in the fish sauce before placing it in their mouths. Jan and I tried.

'Why do you knead the *nshima* so much before eating it?' I asked, but they just laughed and I never received a satisfactory answer.

After lunch we walked some distance to the church and I preached a simple message, encouraging the people to fix their eyes on Jesus and set their minds and hearts on things above. It started to rain and as the noise on the tin roof increased, I stopped preaching. Everyone automatically prayed and soon the atmosphere in the church was one of great freedom, as people repented and did business with God. In the evening I taught on listening to God and the people were very appreciative. They were blessed beyond belief. Teaching must have been rare in that place.

We slept in the house of a pastor, on mattresses on the floor. Before we left, an old lady from the church brought us a traditionally made clay jar and a tea pot with decorative engravings on the outside. 'Lord, don't let them break,' I prayed. We were also given a live duck. Mark Kaoma yanked it up by the feet and I felt sorry for it, so I carried it under my arm, stroking its back to calm it down.

We caused a stir as we walked to Kazembe centre to wait for our transport back to Kawambwa. Mark Kaoma started playing the guitar and we sang. A crowd appeared, watching and listening. A little girl came up to me. 'Can you be my mummy?' she asked in perfect English.

I was shocked. 'Don't you have a mummy?'

'Yes I do, but I want to come with you.'

I laughed. 'Not today. Sorry.'

We arrived back in Kawambwa just before dark and walked to the school. Travelling was very time-consuming and energy-draining in those remote areas, but thankfully the pace of life was fairly slow. We sat down to enjoy the duck, which Vera had prepared for supper.

The next morning, Mark and Bupe received a telephone message from Timothy Chilufya who had just returned from America. 'He told us to cancel your programme here so that you can minister in Ndola, where he lives. He wants you to travel as soon as possible. How about tomorrow?'

'Yes, that sounds fine,' I told them and whispered the word 'flexibility' in Jan's ear.

That evening, Bupe arranged a meeting for the teachers' wives. We squeezed into the lounge of a teacher's house. I gave a short word about the woman from Samaria whom Jesus met at the well. Jan shared a testimony. God showed me the specific healing needs of one woman. A gasp went up from the ladies, as they knew only too well how much she had been suffering. I laid hands on her and prayed and everyone knew God was in that place. Six out of the seven unbelievers repented of their sins and gave their lives to Jesus. They were sad to hear that we were leaving the next day.

'I'll come back later this year with a team,' I assured them.

Early the next morning, the headmaster gave us a lift into Kawambwa. We hoped for transport to Kazembe that day. There we would catch a bus to Mansa. If all went well, it would be a two-day journey to Ndola, a town in the Copper Belt of Zambia. Bupe gave us the name of someone in Mansa where we could spend the night.

We waited for a long time in Kawambwa trading centre. We met a lady Bupe knew. She had some problems. Jan began to explain the gospel to her, but even with Bupe translating, her mind was in such a state of confusion that she could not comprehend anything. Bupe stopped us short. 'She needs deliverance,' he told us.

'We'll leave her with you,' we said.

After waiting for transport for nearly three hours, we went into the Indian shop to buy drinks and said goodbye to our friends.

'Where are you going now?' they asked.

'Ndola. But we have to stop at Mansa for a night and get the bus from there.'

'Wait a minute,' the Indian lady said, and walked out of the door behind the counter. She came back with good news. 'One of my sons is travelling to Mansa today. He can take you if you like.'

Jan and I were delighted at how the Lord had worked out our transport. We didn't even have to stop at Kazembe. We waited for half an hour until the man was ready and climbed into the back of the pick-up, covering ourselves with cloths to protect our skin from the burning wind and sun. We dozed and prayed while they drove for two and a half hours. 'That was quick,' said Jan as we jumped out of the pick-up and stretched.

In Mansa the people we had been directed to were away. Two young nieces were staying in their house. We knew no one else in the town so they agreed to let us sleep there, offering us a narrow bed. Exhausted from all the activity, we covered ourselves with our sheets. That night, we were dive-bombed by swarms of hungry mosquitoes, sampling the delicacy of *muzungu* blood. 'Mosquitoes don't say goodnight; they say good bite,' said Jan.

At 7.00 a.m. we caught the bus to Ndola. After travelling for a few hours, we heard a loud bang by the front left-hand wheel. The bus stopped and someone inspected the damage. None of the passengers knew what had happened, and we continued on our way for another three hours before stopping at an isolated petrol station. The bus conductor announced, 'We're having a twenty-minute break.' Everybody got out and sat under a temporary shelter made of leaves.

We waited, and waited, and waited. After three hours, Jan and I decided to ask the driver what was going on. 'The brakes failed,' he told us, 'and someone's gone to Ndola to get a spare part, but he won't be back till late. So get ready to spend the night here,' he said with a smirk. Jan and I looked around. There were no buildings in sight. At least we had sleeping bags and could sleep on the ground in the open.

'You mean, that bang we heard was the brakes failing and we travelled on for three hours with no brakes?' we pondered.

We walked over to the garage to see if they sold bottled water. 'Look!' said Jan, pointing to a Zambian man who I vaguely recognised. She sprinted over to him and came back with good news. He was one of the workers at the Indian shop in Kawambwa, accompanying his boss to Ndola. The Indian appeared. 'Want a lift?' he asked. 'Get your bags.'

We piled into his pick-up and set off, arriving late in Ndola. He took us to the deserted bus station. People had heard that the bus wouldn't arrive till the following day.

'Where does this Timothy live?' the Indian asked.

'I don't know,' I mumbled. 'All I have is his neighbour's phone number. Where can we phone from?'

'I'll drop you at a hotel,' he told us, and we thanked him for his help.

In the plush reception of the New Savoy Hotel, Jan relaxed in the entrance while I tried to phone. After several attempts, I got through and the neighbour promised to pass on the message to Timothy. 'I hope she does,' I said to Jan. 'Phew!' I flopped on to the most comfortable chair I had sat on for months, and within minutes we were both fast asleep.

An hour later we were woken by Timothy's cheerful voice. We greeted him sleepily and went outside. I watched to see which car we would put our suitcases in. We followed him across the road, down a corridor and up some stairs. He knocked at the door of a flat. 'This is where you'll be staying, with Mrs Banda,' Timothy told us.

Of all the hotels in town, we had stopped at the one opposite the flat where we would be staying.

We were kept busy the whole week in Christian Unions, lunch-time office meetings, people's homes, schools, churches, youth groups, ladies' meetings and a nurses' fellowship. Jan and I preached once, twice or even three times a day.

'We need your ministry here,' was Timothy's comment.

'I'm already praying about coming back,' I told him. I remembered the words that Johnson had prophesied in Uganda the previous year, saying that God had a work for me to do in Zambia. I was beginning to see this fulfilled.

In our spare moments we swam in the hotel pool. As I lay sunbathing, I noticed an American family arriving wearily. They ordered food and drinks and their two children played in the water. Having not spoken to white people for a few weeks, I went over to talk to them.

'We're missionaries from Zaïre,' the lady told me. 'We had to evacuate our home because of the fighting in our village. Our bags have been packed and kept by the front door for several weeks. Our children are used to coming inside daily when the gunfire becomes too much. Our house has been completely ransacked. Absolutely everything was taken, including the toilet, the light switches and light fittings. My husband is a pilot and we live beside the airstrip, so we got in our plane and fled to Zambia. We've just arrived now.'

'What do you think you'll do?' I inquired.

'We'll rest here for a bit and then go to America and decide what to do from there.'

Just then her husband came over with his map in his hand. I invited them to visit us one evening in Mrs Banda's flat where we talked and prayed together.

Before this trip, I had met David Ndarahutse in England. 'If you go to Zambia, you must come to Burundi,' he insisted. 'It's a short boat ride up Lake Tanganyika. Come and see us, even if it's only for a few days.' We decided to take up his offer.

'We have to travel up to the north of Zambia again,' I told Timothy.

We got out a small map. 'This road is impassable. If I were you, I wouldn't travel by road. You can fly up to Kasama,' he suggested, 'and then travel by road from there.'

Our budget didn't stretch to an extra flight.

'Come on. You are women of God. Why not believe Him to provide?' Timothy encouraged, as if he knew what we were thinking.

'Yes,' we agreed, rising to the challenge. 'Let's expect God to do something.'

The very next day, Jan received a letter from a friend, telling her that she had put £100 into Jan's bank account. Timothy went to the airline office where we were put on a waiting list as the eleventh and twelfth people, but we needed to get to the north of Zambia to catch the boat, which left only once a week.

'I'd like to see the senior manager,' Timothy said and was shown to his office. 'These people are servants of

God. It's important they get on that flight,' Timothy insisted. The manager agreed and we somehow jumped the queue.

On our last night we visited Pastor Shawa and his family and sang Bemba songs together. 'Why don't you sing that song, "There is no glory in my own wisdom",' Timothy requested. He was always drawing the best out of us, pushing us forward in a most encouraging way. As I sang, the presence of God surrounded us all. Then the Lord spoke to Jan and me about the members of the family, and we prayed for each one. 'You have a great work ahead of you,' I told one of the daughters. 'God is going to take you through a training process and many will be saved through you.' We left the house quite late but everyone had been blessed.

The next day Timothy met the pastor. 'We stayed up for hours after you left, discussing the prophetic words and we prayed until the early hours of the morning,' the pastor told him. 'And you know the word about evangelism training which was given for my daughter? Well, she has recently been offered a scholarship to go abroad to Bible College, so that's a real confirmation.'

It was sad to say goodbye to Timothy and his wife Kunda but they were excited at the prospect of me coming back with a team later on in the year. We flew to Mansa and then to Kasama, travelling by road to Mbala where Timothy had put us in touch with an organisation called World Vision. They organised a women's seminar and invited leading ladies from different denominations. Jan and I were tired after the non-stop ministry. I had preached every day for a complete month, sometimes two or three times. But we taught in the ladies' seminar and many gave their lives to the Lord.

We enjoyed the green town of Mbala with the fresh-smelling eucalyptus trees. One afternoon we followed a sloping track which led to a small lake surrounded by reeds and bullrushes. Some large drops of rain landed on us and we ran to shelter in the terrace of a nearby house, anticipating a downpour. A friendly lady was sitting on the steps of the house.

'My name's Gladys and I live in Lusaka. I'm here visiting my mother. What are you doing here?' she questioned.

'We're teaching the Bible in a ladies' meeting,' we told her.

'Can you preach to me now?' she requested, and so began my second preach of the day. She gave her life to the Lord and we sang some Bemba praise songs. She was really touched by the love of God and we walked back up the hill praising Jesus.

A kind gentleman drove us to Mpulungu and took us to the port. There was a problem with our booking which I let the Zambians handle while we had lunch with a Christian bank manager. Everything was put in order and we boarded and explored the boat which was to be our new home for the next three days. Sitting on the top deck, I couldn't help noticing how healthy and suntanned the tourists looked compared to the two of us, who were pale and rather underweight.

The lake was a deep blue-green colour. On one side the Tanzanian mountains could be seen, covered with grass and trees; on the other side were the mountains of Zaïre. The cloud formations were interesting, and looked as if they hung on an invisible string at exactly the same height. The tranquillity was occasionally disturbed by bulging boats packed with people throwing their wares up in unofficial trade, all accompanied by the seemingly necessary hollering.

Jan came back from talking to an American couple. 'I can't believe how closed these people are to the gospel. Some don't even want to listen.'

Fifteen Australians were travelling with an overland truck, visiting tourist attractions and game parks. I chatted to one girl who was delighted when she heard I was a Christian. 'I'm the only one in my group and I'm finding it so tough. Most of them get drunk at night. My sister is here but she's not a Christian, so she's joining in with everything they do and I feel so left out. They often tease me as if I'm strange.'

I encouraged her with stories of what had been happening on our mission. 'What exactly is a word of knowledge?' she asked.

'When a person is close to God, sometimes He gives supernatural knowledge about a situation or about another person. For example, God may show me that you have something wrong with your knee.'

'I do have a problem with my knee-cap,' she interrupted, amazed.

'Maybe God wants me to pray for you so you can be healed.'

'Not here,' she said, glancing over at her friends.

'Well, we don't have to close our eyes and make a spectacle of ourselves. We can pray just as if we're talking.'

'OK,' she agreed.

Life on the boat was good. Everyone was friendly. We made the most of our free time, reading the Bible, writing letters and catching up on sleep. In the cafe, the food was reasonable. Jan and I had a cabin to ourselves, which became hot and stuffy and we often woke up sweating. At least there were showers on the boat. It was good for us to catch up with each other. We had been so occupied with activity that I hadn't even heard what God had been doing in her life since we set foot in Africa. 'I'll never be the same again,' she told me.

On the second day of our boat journey, we stopped at Kigoma in Tanzania and walked around the town. We had a meal, bought some fruit and even witnessed to some of the people. We swam in Lake Tanganyika and washed our hair. The locals were amused when they saw our bubbly shampoo floating on the surface as we dived under the water to rinse off.

In the early hours of the third morning, I realised something was different. The chugging of the engine had stopped. From my bunk bed I looked out of the window. I could see the Burundi mountains sparkling, lights dotted around the city. It was a unique sight. We had arrived in beloved Burundi, the place of peace.

By daylight we entered the dock. I was pleased to see Edmond, David's nephew, waiting for us at the port. He had come to sort out our visas. That meant they must have received our letter. We hugged him and asked how everything was.

'David left for America yesterday, so you've missed him.' He saw the disappointment on my face. 'Sorry about that,' he said sympathetically. 'How about staying with us?' Jan and I were delighted to spend time with Edmond, his wife Faith and their children.

We rested, swam and visited many of my friends. 'Aren't these people lovely?' Jan commented one day.

'Yes, I think the environment is good for people here. It's easier to get the priorities in the right order. Instead of being preoccupied with achieving goals and having possessions, people are considered important. Have you heard that saying: 'Love people and use things; don't love things and use people'? The slower pace of life enables people to give others more time,' I reasoned. It was such a blessing to be showing Jan around.

'I only read about this place in your letters, but it's even more beautiful than I imagined,' she told me.

After a week in Burundi, we flew to Nairobi in time for the crusade and leaders' meeting where Pastor Yonggi Cho was ministering. 'What a great way to round up a wonderful trip!' we agreed.

Having been on the road for seven months, we flew back to England, arriving on a grey, drizzly morning. Jan wrote down her first impressions:

The newspapers bring back the horror of this dark age – the West with all its psychological problems and crazy obsessions. Satan's having a blast with the materialistic world. In Africa the issues are life and death; the next meal; water; the fight against poverty; sickness and war; theft and mob violence – down-to-earth stuff. Here it's mind games; gossip; obsession with the body; the career; finances and leisure time. People are trapped in mental torments, meaningless pursuits and despair. This country needs Christ as much as Africa.

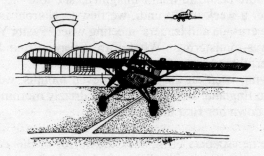

9

Ride on the Heights

Why should I anticipate the worst
when God has always given me the best?

Peace and quiet at last! I shut myself away in my room,
desperately wanting time with the Lord. I sang the song I
had written a few days before:

> Jesus, I want to be like You,
> Like You in every way.
> Jesus, I want to be like You,
> Like You every day.

Perfect in all of Your ways,
Wise in all that You do and say,
Holy and blameless and pure,
Lord, I want to be like You.

You're full of power and love,
Authority from the Father above,
Willing to heal and to save,
Lord, I want to be like You.

I was soon lost in wonder of the beauty of Jesus Christ the Saviour. My thoughts were taken up with Him and the warmth and comfort of His love surrounded me as I knelt on the floor.

'You've got to learn to fly,' were the words I heard.

I looked around to see where the voice had come from. Learn to fly? Fly a plane? Me – learn to fly? I started to laugh and said, 'Lord, is that You?' Then, remembering how Abraham's wife, Sarah, had laughed in unbelief at the thought of bearing a child in her old age, I quickly said, 'OK, I believe You, Lord. But You know my financial situation. If this is really You, please confirm it to me.'

After that experience, several months went by, but the words would not leave me. Every time I saw a light aircraft flying overhead, I was reminded of the event and a sense of peace confirmed that it must be God's plan. Flying a small plane in Africa would certainly be an asset to the ministry.

Coming home from my trip with Jan, I promptly looked through the Yellow Pages. I had no idea what it entailed to learn to fly. I had certainly never imagined myself doing such a thing. After church one day, a young man asked me, 'What are you doing now you're back from Africa?'

I began to laugh. 'You'll never believe it, but I'm going to learn to fly.' It all seemed so far-fetched to me.

'Oh, really?' he said, sounding very interested. 'A friend of mine is the owner of a flying school down in Shoreham, and he owes me a favour. I lent him my racing car and he said in return he'd teach me to fly at a discount price. But flying isn't my thing. Maybe he can do it for you instead. I'll phone and ask him.'

He phoned me the next day, saying his friend was very willing to do this favour for me. I booked a trial flight and drove to the airport in a car which God had provided for me to use for the next three months. After much prayer and excitement, I experienced my first flight. I thoroughly enjoyed it and knew this must be the Lord's will. My instructor was very encouraging and friendly, which I felt was important. If he'd been the kind to rebuke me severely at every little mistake, I knew I would never succeed.

The Private Pilot's Licence requires a minimum of forty hours' flying, eleven of which must be solo (with no one else in the two-seater Cessna), and three hours of flying on instruments only, with no peeping out of the window. There are four thick volumes of information, plus the Aviation Law flight rules and procedures to assimilate. It entails passing seven multiple-question written exams. Towards the end there is a general flying exam involving various manoeuvres such as stalling the plane, forced landings and low flying, then a cross-country trip to prove navigation skills, and finally a solo cross-country flight, landing away at another airport.

Several years earlier, before I went to Roffey Place, I was left an inheritance by my great-aunt. When I received it, I said to the Lord, 'This is Your money. What do You want me to do with it?' He had told me to save it for the future, to be used for flights. I had assumed it would be used for commercial flights, but now I saw exactly what the Lord had meant.

I intended to stay in England and obtain the Private Pilot's Licence before going back to Africa again. I thought about getting a secretarial job for a few months to earn enough money to complete the flying course before I actually started. When I saw Colin Urquhart, I told him what was happening. 'Just go ahead with the money you already have and God will provide the rest,' he advised. 'The Father provides for the child, not the other way round.' I took this as a promise from God and went ahead with the lessons.

One day, the instructor turned to me as we queued to take off. 'In my professional opinion, you're ready for your first solo landing. Go for it! Take off, do the circuit just like you've been doing with me, and come down to land. I'll be sitting on the grass here, watching your landing.' He opened the door of the plane and jumped out.

'Help!' was my first reaction. 'Well, Lord, I'm glad You're still here with me,' I said out loud, lining up for take-off. And God certainly helped me. I did the best landing I think I have ever done, much to the delight of the instructor.

'Congratulations!' he said, shaking my hand heartily. 'After only twelve and a half hours of flying, you did excellently. You've made my day – no, you've made my week!'

Touch and go's were great fun, too. After coming in to land, instead of applying the brakes, you give it full throttle and take off again, flying the circuit and landing and taking off again. I spent many happy hours practising and shouting with delight on each landing. It was particularly fun bumping along on a grassy runway before having a rapid lift-off.

The time came for me to do my first cross-country solo flight. A few minutes after take-off, I was horrified to notice that the fuel gauges were rapidly going down. Oh no! Perhaps there was a leak, or maybe the man who had just fuelled the plane had forgotten to put the lids back on the two tanks in the wings. I spotted the grassy runway at Goodwood below and contacted the control tower to ask for advice. They suggested that I land and check it out, which would incur a landing fee of around £10. At about two hundred feet from the ground, the tower radioed me to say that my instructor had just telephoned with the message that I should return immediately to Shoreham. So I made a quick changeabout and started the ascent up to the usual flying level back towards Shoreham. It was a relief to land and find that the fuel had not run out, although the left gauge had been on empty for several minutes. I later discovered that the man at the pump had not tightened the lid sufficiently for the pressure in the tank to give a correct reading.

It didn't take long for all my money to be used up. 'I won't be able to come next week,' I told my instructor.

'Oh, why is that?' he asked.

'OK, I'll be honest with you. I've completely run out of money, but I'm believing God for a miracle. I've been living like this for a number of years and God has always provided everything I've needed, so I know He'll do it again.'

'Well, just give us a ring when you want to come,' he said, looking at me intently.

'See you soon!' I said, as I smiled and walked away.

It was a welcome rest. I had been doing two flights a day and studying each evening. The house had been quiet because Mum and Dad were in Uganda. They were helping to raise funds for the Miracle Centre Orphanage in the war-torn Luwero district. When Robert Kayanja preached there in the early '90s he had found many orphans sleeping in the bush, surviving on wild fruits and roots. He knew something had to be done for them and the work was begun. Being retired teachers, Mum and Dad took up the challenge and visited Uganda for a couple of months each year to help in the running of the school and to teach and love the children.

My whole life had been taken up with flying. It was like living in the middle of a miracle. I had been driving to the airport in a borrowed car and spending an average of £200 a day, which seemed ridiculous compared to my usual lifestyle. But anyway, it was God's money.

My brother Adrian was keenly interested in the flying and asked me why I was not going to Shoreham that week.

'Well, as you've asked, I'll tell you. I'm completely out of money, but I know God's going to do something.'

I also told Jan about the situation. But I would never ask anyone for money. This was God's idea and I had confidence that somehow He would provide. After a week, when still no money had come and I had eaten frozen peas and marrow from the garden for two days, I asked the Lord, 'Should I be battling in prayer? Maybe You want me to fast?'

'No, I'll do it,' He assured me.

Then the miracles started happening. After only a week, someone came to me with three blank, signed cheques saying that God had told him to pay for my next three lessons. 'Do you know how much I'm paying each day?' I exclaimed.

'I've got an idea, but this is what God has told me to do.' I told him how much it was costing. 'Even if it's more, that's OK,' was his reply.

You should have seen the instructor's eyes as I wrote

out those cheques. 'This is typical of what God does. He's brilliant!' I boasted.

Those guys running the flying school were great. My prayer was that they would come to know God personally. They were certainly impressed by the weather conditions that year. 'Well, I do have a close relationship with the Higher Authority,' I said, looking up to the sky. Once, I decided to take two days off to study. The weather was so abysmal that no one could fly for those two days anyway. The day I came back, it was bright and crisp with not a cloud in the sky.

Money seemed to be coming in from everywhere. A friend wrote to me for the first time in two years and enclosed a cheque for £200. Others gave cash and more cheques kept coming from various quarters. Yet I had not told anyone of my need, apart from the Lord. £3,000 passed through my hands in a space of two months. 'Well, if that's not God, I don't know what is!' I told Jan.

After several hours of work, concentration and study, I passed all the exams and acquired my Private Pilot's Licence. Glory to God! That was one adventure I will never forget. I am still waiting to see the fulfilment of God's intention for me to fly.

10

So I am Sending You

It's time we stopped being oppressed and started oppressing the devil in Jesus' name

In September 1993, I went back to Zambia with a team of seven. We bought our tickets for less than half price, an encouraging miracle to start the trip. Ali, Gerry and I travelled for twelve hours by air and were met at Lusaka Airport by a beaming Timothy Chilufya. It was good to see him again and catch up on all the news. We boarded a bus to Ndola, discovering when we set off that there was no glass in our window, so Ali and I suffered a very windy, nine-hour journey. We faxed the rest of the team in England, advising them to take the plane to Ndola if possible, when they joined us in a few days' time.

Timothy arranged a great two-week schedule of ministry around the Ndola area in schools, colleges, churches and lunch-time fellowships. It was wonderful. Everyone had a chance to preach, many for the first time, and the Zambians were always responsive and so grateful to hear the Word of God. In one school a hundred pupils were saved!

In each place, Timothy spoke before introducing the team. He told us of the time when he had been due to fly somewhere urgently. He booked his ticket, but didn't have all the money needed. He felt restless the night before, as he had no idea where the money would come from. The problem weighed heavily on him. As he prayed that evening, he read Job 5:22: 'You will laugh at destruction and famine.' Laughter welled up within him, as he remembered what a mighty God we have. He laughed in the face of the need, believing that God would do something. In the morning he went to the airport and stood in the queue, still with no money. As the person in front of him reached the counter, he felt like going home. But the Lord assured him not to give up, and suddenly a man came out of a side door. 'Timothy! Praise God! How are you? I've just returned from America. Here . . .' and the friend thrust some money into his hand. It was just the right amount, and Timothy boarded the plane, rejoicing in God's marvellous ways.

Timothy spoke of another occasion when one of his daughters was taken seriously ill. They had called a doctor, but nothing could be done. The girl's body turned stiff and her eyes rolled back.

'Well, you know what we've got to do,' Timothy's wife

Kunda said. 'We must laugh at destruction.'

'Oh no, honey! That's too much. Not in this situation, surely?' Timothy reasoned.

'Well, I'm going to obey God anyway,' said Kunda, and she started to laugh. At first it felt false, but she laughed in faith and Timothy soon joined her, 'Ha ha ha! You devil, you're not going to take our daughter, ha ha ha, Jesus defeated you on the cross. Ha, ha, hee, hee, hallelujah, thank You, Lord, for the victory. Glory!' They laughed and laughed for hours into the night. The body of the girl was restored and by the morning there was no trace of the sickness.

Whenever people heard this story, faith was inspired in their hearts.

'Don't let your needs and your problems bind your spirit,' Timothy said. 'Laugh in the face of what the devil may try to do, laugh in the face of poverty, laugh at those stubborn situations. As you release your spirit to God, His power can bring the change you need. Go ahead,' he encouraged. 'Laugh! Rejoice in God.' Sometimes, the place would erupt with laughter for several minutes and the Lord moved, meeting needs and healing and delivering His people.

In the third week, we travelled to the small town of Mansa. I will never forget what happened on the Saturday. After several teaching sessions, Timothy called people forward for prayer. Before we knew it, Sharron had run to lay hands on them and they were all falling down under the power of God. Then she told me she had seen a vision of four young men who God was going to use mightily as evangelists. We picked them out of the crowd. Sharron and I held hands with them in a circle and closed our eyes to pray. Before we had spoken two sentences to the Lord, I felt my hands being pulled as the men suddenly fell to the floor. Sharron and I looked at each other, astounded. God was on the move. We prophesied to the young men as they lay there.

Everyone sang and rejoiced in the presence of God. The atmosphere was electric. There was so much joy as we danced before the Lord, moving among the beautiful people of Zambia.

Later Sharron asked me, 'Did I do the right thing?' She had never prayed for people before; she had never preached or led anyone to the Lord, but she surrendered to God. 'Yeah, you're flowing with the Holy Spirit, girlie. Keep going – it's great!'

The events which had led to Sharron coming to Zambia were supernatural. We met at Kingdom Faith's annual camp one year and she asked me what I was doing. When I told her how God was moving in Africa it set her thinking about her life and how many people she was affecting for eternity. Later, she left her nursing job for three months to go to Roffey Place Bible College where God did a wonderful work in her life. Towards the end of the term, the students sought God concerning what they would do next.

I went to see Colin, to tell him of my plans to take a team to Zambia. Immediately I left his office, Sharron came to see him.

'Well, what has the Lord been saying to you?' was his opening line.

'Some very strange things have been happening recently,' Sharron began. 'I thought I heard God speak to me in an audible voice. He said, "Zambia". That's a country in Africa, isn't it? I don't know anything about Zambia and I don't know anyone there.'

'How about staying in a mud hut with Anthea?' Colin said. After some discussion, he concluded, 'Leave it with me and I'll come back to you.'

Meanwhile, I had cycled home, and arrived to hear the phone ringing. It was Colin. He told me the story and asked me what I thought. It sounded great to me. So Sharron came to Zambia in faith, knowing that God was sending her for a specific purpose. The evidence was already plain to see.

After two weeks, Ali and Gerry left us in Mansa and travelled back to England. The rest of the group journeyed further north to a village called Lukwesa. The 'Lukwesa experience' is still mentioned in our conversations today for reasons which you will soon understand.

There was great excitement as we got off the bus. People seemed to appear from nowhere, offering to carry our luggage. Escorted by about fifty locals, we walked along the main road and down a little dirt track leading to the village. We arrived at a brick house which had been used as an office. There was even electricity. The girls slept in one room and the boys in another, with the concrete floor as our communal bed. I put some clothes underneath my sleeping bag to cushion myself a bit.

Outside the house, there was so much noise. What on earth was happening? I looked up at the window. Seven kids were staring in on one side and eight clamouring in the opposite window. About a hundred and fifty children had gathered to see the *muzungus*. Claire hung up a piece of cloth as a makeshift curtain. At least we could stop some of the staring, if not the noise. 'How long are we staying here?' I wondered. Only a week, I hoped.

This was the first Spirit-filled crusade ever to take place in Lukwesa. For generations, the only religion had been demon-worship and witchcraft. 'Don't be afraid of the witchcraft,' Timothy encouraged us. 'They'll see the fire of God over the house and won't be able to do a thing.'

Among the population of thirty thousand, there were only two small churches – and no running water and only one electricity wire. The churches came together for this event. One pastor had moved to the village two years ago with his wife and seven children. They had a small congregation of about twenty new believers. I asked some questions to test their spiritual temperature and found that they knew about the blood of Jesus and the cleansing of their sin, but they didn't know much else.

On the first evening we had an open-air meeting. It was a difficult start. As soon as the presence of God was felt, demons manifested. People rolled around in the dust, causing a great commotion. However, Mark continued preaching, declaring that the light of Jesus Christ had come to dispel the darkness. I felt that our success would be in teaching the Christians; our efforts would produce lasting results if they were established in the truth. They desperately needed to be fed with the Word of God.

That night, Sharron and I went down to the river to wash under the starry sky. We walked along the shore with grateful hearts, feeling privileged to be in such a beautiful place for the sake of the gospel. 'Ah! What's that!' Sharron screamed as we nearly stepped on a man sleeping in the undergrowth. We walked back quickly with images of crocodiles running through our minds.

I really needed to pray, but I felt so tired and sleep was beckoning. As I put my head down on my makeshift pillow and closed my eyes, I saw a skull zooming in towards my face. I laughed out loud and said, 'Satan, you can't scare me,' and then turned over and went to sleep.

Early in the morning everyone was up. Once again, crowds of children had gathered to see us brushing our teeth. Of course, there was no sink with running water, so everything had to be done openly. We made our way down to the river, soap and towel in hand. Cries went out over the village: 'The *muzungus* are going to wash.' We heard the pounding of footsteps as children and adults ran to see this great phenomenon. As we swam, they were astounded to see us floating on the water, thinking we were using special powers to do so. Not many of the locals were able to swim, even though they lived by the river. We counted 136 people on the river bank. Here was a captive audience. Someone suggested that we preach from the water, but we decided to save our energy for the busy day ahead.

We returned to the house to find Mark down with malaria. Timothy had some drugs and Sharron, being a qualified nurse, administered the injections. It was still early, but the sun was already beating on the tin roof of the house and the heat was stifling. None of us had been able to sleep very well. Claire and Sharron had heard the guitar playing on its own in our room. One of the Zambians sharing the room with us had been praying and interceding most of the night. It seemed that various activities had been taking place, as some of us heard chanting.

I had never been anywhere quite like this before. I told Timothy, 'Next time you bring us to such a village, please give us some warning so we can fast and pray beforehand.' We had just finished two busy weeks of non-stop ministry and were not in the best position, physically or spiritually, to fight effectively in this environment. Nevertheless, God was with us and we were not going to give up until the good news had been brought to the people of Lukwesa.

The seminar started at 9.00 a.m. and carried on until 5.00 p.m. with no break in the middle. We taught and ministered for an hour or two each, and the teaching was broken up by times of praise and prayer. Just before I preached one day, a man stood up speaking loudly in Bemba. Not understanding what he was saying, I went ahead and preached. Afterwards, Timothy told me that he was complaining about our conference, explaining that in a dream God showed him that we were achieving nothing in Lukwesa. When I heard this, I leapt for joy and laughed. The opposition indicated that God was about to do something powerful. The people of Lukwesa were so hungry for spiritual food. They sat listening for hours on the edge of their chairs, their eyes beaming, drinking from the Word of life. Those who could write took extensive notes on the paper we supplied.

I returned to the house after preaching. 'Is there any drinking water?' I gasped. There was none left, so I waited while they collected it from the river and boiled it over firewood. The only alternative was to drink water from my little hand pump filter, which tasted disgusting. Often, there was no drinking water in the house. I wished our friends could understand that we desperately needed to drink in this intense heat. There was no shop where we could buy the limited selection of fizzy drinks available in other places. Many of us were suffering from diarrhoea and had to make frequent visits to 'cockroach city', as Sharron and Claire called the infested pit latrine.

One day, when I was preaching the message of faith, I suddenly felt terribly ill. I persevered but in the end I had to cut the message short. I found Sharron back at the house. 'I feel as if I've got malaria. Can we go and find that clinic?'

We walked for twenty minutes in the hot midday sun, my temperature soaring. I was so dizzy, I could hardly put one foot in front of another. Sharron linked her arm in mine and prayed until we arrived at the crowded clinic. I sat down on a chair and waited.

'Sharron, I suddenly feel completely better,' I said.

The nurse took my temperature. 'Malaria? No, you don't even have a high temperature.'

I put my hand to my head. All the heat had gone. 'The devil is a liar. He's just trying to stop the Word of God going out,' I said.

Many children in that remote village had massive open wounds and ulcers on their legs. People would bring their babies, dying of malnutrition. I will never forget the sight of a little girl screaming in agony as her mother roughly removed the leaves which had stuck to the raw flesh on her leg. They had been placed there in an attempt to keep the flies and dirt out.

'Most of these children will either lose their limbs or die from infection unless God does a miracle,' Sharron told us. 'The wounds would not have developed so much if they had been cleaned immediately with boiled water; they might have even healed up.'

With love and tender care, she bathed the children's decayed limbs and ulcerous wounds, dressed them with what we could find in our own first aid kit and prayed. I'm not a squeamish sort of person but the suffering in that place was immense. I was amazed that these parents didn't take their children to the clinic for treatment.

'This place is a nurse's nightmare,' said Sharron. 'It's easier when you're ignorant. We're breaking so many rules, but some things can't be avoided.' She wrote in her diary:

My heart was quite broken today and I cried. I felt so empty, so helpless. The poverty here is awful. The people run around in rags and their faces are so sad. They are malnourished too and their skin is in bad condition with marks all over. There's horrible witchcraft here; the people are bound. I cried to God today like I haven't in a long time. 'Lord, heal and liberate these suffering children. Lord, release Your power and let Your Kingdom come.'

One morning Timothy told me soberly, 'I've just received a message that my brother is very sick and about to die.' He had been ill with one sickness, but was taken to the local witchdoctor who gave him dirty water to drink. So now he had dysentery as well. He lived in the far north of Zambia. 'I want to go and pray for him,' said Timothy. My heart sank. Oh no, the army was being depleted. Mark was out of action, and now Timothy wanted to leave us here alone for two days. Well, of course he had to go. We waved him off. 'Don't be too long,' I urged. Timothy himself was not very well. A boil had come up on his neck under the skin. This was a tough place to be in. Yet we were only here for one week. What about the pastor, whose children kept getting sick? He and his wife looked very discouraged when we first arrived. Everything was hard here. Praying was becoming a near-impossible task, partly due to lack of privacy. I thought of the verse in Job 5: 'You shall laugh at destruction and famine.'

I felt the sentence of death over us as a group. The forces of darkness wanted us out of that place, but we refused to move, no matter what. I knew God would preserve us and save many people. We were leaving a mark on that village for eternity. At times like this I felt the harshness of the cross. Jesus said, 'If anyone would come after me, he must deny himself and take up his cross daily and follow me.' In past seasons I had discovered that to run away from the cross was more painful than embracing it. I had to daily lay down my life for Jesus, who had shown His great love for me. His grace was sufficient in any situation He led me into and He would only allow me to pass through circumstances for which He had thoroughly prepared me. Instead of devastating me, these times brought strength and understanding.

A pastor who lived on the Zaïrean side of the river heard about the crusade and seminar. He came over eagerly by boat each day. On the fourth day, I spoke to him and realised that he'd been unable to communicate with anyone, not knowing English or Bemba. He had sat in the meetings, watching the proceedings without understanding what was going on. He was delighted to discover I spoke French. In fact I was the only one in the village with whom he could communicate. We rowed over the river to visit his family. He gave us one of the doves he had been rearing. Unfortunately, it escaped from Sharron's hands, and we were given a chicken instead which travelled with us in the boat.

The climax of the week was the day we all taught on different aspects of the Holy Spirit. He was poured out in such a beautiful and awesome way. When we started praying for the people, sudden rain pelted loudly on the tin roof, the first rain in several weeks. As we finished praying the rain stopped as abruptly as it had begun.

When I prayed for one man, demons came out of him and he fell to the floor with a bang, but stood up in peace, his face radiant with the glory of God. He came to the front to speak. I noticed people's wide-eyed stares; silence fell on everyone. Our interpreter translated. 'Many of you have heard of me. I am a witchdoctor from the next village. A week ago, a Christian came to my house and preached the gospel. I repented and from that time I tried to tell people about Jesus. There were no Christians in my village. When I came to Lukwesa to buy paraffin, I heard the preaching and ran in here. And now I've received the Holy Spirit.'

The people were stunned, still afraid of his witchcraft.

'God has power to transform lives completely,' Timothy began. (He had returned from his visit to his brother.) 'Why are you afraid of this man? Whatever God does, He does thoroughly. This man is going to become a pastor. He will start by leading a church in his home, and will win many people to the Lord.' Turning to the man, Timothy said, 'When sick people come to you to be treated through your witchcraft, preach to them and lay your hands on them like this.' He demonstrated. 'Heal them in the name of Jesus.' Everybody clapped.

'Do you still have your witchcraft materials?' Timothy asked.

'Yes,' the man replied. 'I gave them to my father to keep last week when I became born again.'

'Bring them here tomorrow morning and we'll burn them openly. God is going to use you mightily. Receive from Him now!' Timothy laid hands on him. He fell down to the ground and lay there while the meeting continued.

Another man stood up. 'Last night I was visited by two angels who told me to come to the church meeting today. I asked my mother what it meant. She said it was from God. So I came here, and I feel so happy, so free, so . . .'

'Do you know Jesus as your Saviour?' Timothy interrupted.

'I'm so happy, I just . . .'

'Have you asked God to forgive you for your sins?'

The man was overwhelmed, but managed to pray a prayer, handing over his life to God. Everyone rejoiced. I was so pleased that God believed in what we were doing. He even sent angels to the village, which was encouraging as we had been so aware of the demonic forces.

A third man shared his story: 'I've been suffering with a perpetual headache for eight years. I used to travel in the villages preaching the gospel. Then one day, I stood up to preach and felt terrible pains in my head. I stopped speaking and the pains left, but every time I tried to preach the same thing happened. In the end I stopped ministering and I'm ashamed to say that I backslid. From that time on I've had a permanent headache. But now I give God all the glory. I am completely healed. Jesus has forgiven me, and I'm going to use the last years of my life preaching everywhere,' he declared. I was amazed, as when I prayed for him, I had thought it was a simple headache. I shared some scriptures with him to enable him to stand firm in faith and overcome every evil power.

We walked to the river to baptise some of the believers. Mark ran down to the riverside to see Timothy baptising Sharron, who had not been baptised on her conversion a few years previously.

On our last night, I sensed a new peace. Claire was awake most of the night and had heard no chanting.

The time came for us to leave Lukwesa. We packed our bags and walked to the main road to wait for a bus. 'When we get back to civilisation, I'm going to buy at least six bottles of drink,' Claire announced.

'Me too. Boy am I dehydrated!' I replied.

'Rehydrating on Coke! Hmm!' Sharron commented.

Sharron and Claire lay on the benches in the bus shelter, exhausted from the sleepless nights and the heat. I wandered down the road. Suddenly out of the corner of my eye I saw dust and straw sweeping round furiously. I had heard that such whirlwinds could destroy a thatched roof in seconds. I focused my camera, attempting to capture the unusual sight, and took the photo just as a demon-possessed man walked into view, with his rear end exposed.

Back at the bus shelter, some people came to have a last gaze at our white skin. The pastor and his wife, who came to see us off, preached the gospel to the curious villagers, and to their delight led six people to the Lord in a matter of minutes. Timothy's brother-in-law, Chala, stayed behind for a month or two to continue the work in Lukwesa.

Eventually the bus arrived and we boarded, waving goodbye to Mark who was going back to the UK. What a strange sight we must have been: three *muzungus* loaded with luggage, travelling deep into the bush with a chicken and two guinea-pigs which the pastor had given us. Sharron settled the chicken safely on her lap, much to the amusement of the locals. I saw its beady eye staring at a tomato she was holding. The chicken suddenly dived for it and pecked, spurting juice all over Sharron's clothes. We laughed. Poor thing, it must have been dehydrated too!

Some weeks later, two of the most enthusiastic-looking young men from Lukwesa came to see us. They used public transport to travel as far as they could afford to go and then spent hours walking in the hot African sun to reach the conference where we were.

'After you left Lukwesa, we went from house to house throughout the whole village for two weeks spreading the good news. Many were won to the Lord,' they told us.

It had all been worthwhile.

11

To Destroy the Works
of the Evil One

It's the devil's job to attack; our job is to overcome

We headed off for Kawambwa, where Jan and I had spent
two weeks earlier in the year. The original idea was to
plant a church there, but as Timothy's assistant, Bupe,
was in Singapore for a month, we decided to wait until he
returned. When he first moved to Kawambwa Boys'
Secondary School, he started a fellowship which split,
and even that group splintered into another ineffective

piece while the people of Kawambwa remained un-reached. Spiritual maturity was needed in such an environment so that the Kingdom of God could be established.

We started house-to-house evangelism with Mark Kaoma and another man called Chanda, but people were not responding. We felt under pressure to be active, achieving something, but it was like banging our heads against a brick wall. I asked the Lord about it and sensed that more prayer was needed for Kawambwa. We could lay a foundation for those who would follow us in the work of the gospel there.

One Sunday I preached in a small fellowship meeting in a school classroom. 'These people are fairly new believers,' I was told, and found out later that they were from the Presbyterian church where Jan and I had ministered and the whole congregation had been born again. Due to denominational persecution, they had left and established their own ministry.

Our living conditions were a challenge once again. Sharron, Claire and I slept in a row on the concrete floor, together with Isobel, a Zambian lady who had come to set up a restaurant to generate an income for the ministry.

One night, I lay awake, my back aching. I sensed evil and started praying. In the darkness, a bat circled the room. I wondered how it had got through the grate in the ventilation, as there were no windows in our section of the building. Round and round the bat flew, until it landed on Claire's back.

'Eerr!' She awoke suddenly and flapped the bed sheets in the dark, desperately trying to remove it.

Each morning we were forced out of bed early because the sun heated up the iron roof. Every night had its own event. Once, we heard scuffling outside our curtain door.

Sharron shouted to the boys in the next room. They came running, anticipating an emergency. Having found a torch, we were amazed to see a little dog scampering about in the hall. How had it come in? The doors and windows had been shut.

'Hello doggy!' I said. It looked up at me blankly.

'In the name of Jesus, get out!' Mark and Chanda yelled in unison. 'It might be witchcraft,' they told me, once the dog had gone. 'Sometimes people come in the form of different animals to do their mischief. These witches can even transport people from town to town.'

I sensed this could be true. I once heard a story from an English evangelist. One day, while the ministry team were praying, a small bird flew into the room. They continued to pray, binding all powers of darkness. The bird panicked, bashing itself against the ceiling, but managed to escape through the window. The next day, the team were buying souvenirs in the market when a woman walked up to them with her arm in a sling. 'You did this last night,' she declared, pointing to her arm. 'How dare you! We'll get you back.' But, of course, nothing happened. As Proverbs says, 'Like a . . . darting swallow, an undeserved curse does not come to rest.' The blood of Jesus is enough protection from all witchcraft for those who have faith in God.

One day, Sharron was kicking a football around with some of the local children when she twisted her ankle. Her foot clicked loudly and she thought it was broken. She was taken to a clinic where a nurse put it in plaster. Afterwards, Sharron lay around, praying, reading, seeking God and 'ho-ho-ing' at destruction. She felt uneasy, preaching about Jesus for whom nothing is impossible while she limped around with her foot in plaster. She couldn't face standing in front of people to teach and pray for the sick with her leg like this. Besides, it was terrible to be stuck indoors, unable to move.

'That's it! I've had enough. I'm healed in Jesus' name,' she confessed. She caught a lift to the clinic, asked them to take the plaster off and walked the two miles back to the Centre. All the pain had left her foot. Being a nurse she knew what a risk she was taking if God had not done a miracle for her. However, she was led by the Holy Spirit, and indeed God rewarded her faith and obedience.

After a couple of weeks in Kawambwa, we looked for a more comfortable place to stay, to use as a base for the next two months. We saw various mud houses with thatched roofs and found one we liked about five minutes' walk from the Centre. We negotiated a price and spent most of our money on the house, trusting God to provide what we needed for living and travelling. We moved in with nothing, but quickly acquired a few things such as mattresses which some kind Christians lent us when they heard about our needs. We were given plates and cups, and toothbrushes made a good substitute for stirring tea until we found a town where cutlery was sold. 'The way you are living is somewhat awkward,' commented Jones, Bupe's son-in-law.

With satisfaction, I stuck my postcards and pictures on the salmon-pink bedroom wall and hung up a piece of cloth to replace the door, which had been removed by the previous owner. Pleased to enjoy some privacy for the first time in weeks, I whispered, 'It's just me and you again, Lord.' I opened my shutter and watched the setting sun painting the sky orange and pink, and admired the neighbours' ducks waddling around, pecking up food which had been thrown on the ground. I settled down to write in my diary:

Hallelujah! I have to express my thanks to the Lord. We've moved into our house and my room is cosy by candlelight. Dogs are barking and kids crying, drums beating, but I'm content. He satisfies my desires with good things. Praise His holy name!

Early in the morning, we would put charcoal in the round iron cooker, pour on paraffin and set light to it using damp matches. Then we would swing it outside by the handle and hang it on a cassava tree for good ventilation. Passers-by often stopped to stare at the strange sight of a *muzungu* doing such a thing. Someone would walk the two hundred metres from the house to collect the water, usually to find that the supply had already been switched off and there was none coming out of the tap. Thankfully, the lady who lived by the tap usually shared her water with us if we came too late, and even made a point of collecting extra just in case. After all these preparations, it sometimes took an hour to boil water for tea, depending how damp the charcoal was.

We called our home 'the palace' as it was one of its kind in the village. The outside wall was painted dark blue which gave it a royal look, and there were many rooms inside. We swept the floor with a small hand brush made of dried grass and then mopped using my old nightshirt, the only rag we could find. This was a very necessary procedure as bits constantly fell from the thatch, and dust came off the mud walls. There were two separate store cupboards, where we kept the guinea-pigs under lock and key to deprive the thieves of their supper. Meat was very rare in that village! Another room was used as a mud-floor 'bathroom'. We washed in a plastic bowl on the days we didn't walk to the small waterhole to swim and cool off. Outside, we had a beautifully made round

shelter, with a small wall a metre high and poles support-
ing a circular thatched roof. It was lovely to sit there and
feel the breeze.

Some days we had a constant stream of visitors: people
selling eggs, others asking for help and swarms of inquisitive children. Once, when the number of children and their
noise became too much to cope with, having tried in
numerous ways to encourage them to go, I ran out with
Sharron's crutches, putting on an angry face. They all
scattered and I went indoors; smiling as I thought of the
situation and the unusual behaviour it called for on my
part.

It seemed that every time we prayed together, there was
some kind of disturbance. Once we were just entering
into the presence of God when someone started knocking
on the wooden shutter of the window. We attempted to
ignore it, but it persisted so I had to find out who it was.
This happened time and time again, apart from one
morning when we sat together in my room. We shared
communion using locally baked bread rolls and instant
cappuccino coffee which Sharron's mum had sent us
through the post. It was a precious time of prayer and
fellowship and a great encouragement to each of us.

Mark Kaoma invited all churches in the area to join us
for an overnight meeting. We met in the hall, one tiny gas
lamp struggling to give out light. No Christians turned
up, only a crowd of unbelievers who wanted to see what
was happening at Kawambwa Christian Centre. The
singing was rowdy, to say the least. One needed authority
from God in such an unsettled atmosphere. I preached a
simple gospel message, projecting my voice into the
darkness. 'The broad road leads to destruction but God's
narrow road leads to life. Which road are you on?' Seven
teenage boys came forward for salvation, and one was

visibly touched by God's power and fell to the ground. When we met him the next day he told us he had never experienced God's power in such an awesome way.

After the meeting we walked back home in the pitch black. There was no moon or stars; thick rain clouds covered the sky so the narrow path could hardly be seen. We placed each foot down carefully, our eyes straining ahead.

'It's OK, you two,' I reassured my friends. 'I know this bit; there are no puddles here.'

No sooner had these words left my mouth when – splash! I found myself ankle-deep in water. The girls nearly wet themselves laughing. I continued to lead the way and suddenly came face to face in the darkness with a teenage schoolgirl, who stood screaming in terror. We had not seen or heard each other until we were a foot apart. Maybe she thought I was a ghost. It was quite unusual to see a white person in that area.

Our neighbours were really friendly. Sometimes we sat with them, and once we helped them to pound dried cassava into fine powder using a large stick and a hollowed-out log standing up on end. As we walked by one day, a little old lady approached us, wearing a toothless grin and clutching a paper bag in her hands. The girls greeted her and she offered them some termites to eat. Boldly they put some in their mouths and crunched them up.

'Mmm, a bit like crisps,' Sharron commented, reaching for another handful.

I decided my stomach wasn't up to it. 'Oh well,' I thought to myself, 'at least I ate caterpillars the other day.'

The locals soon got to know our names – well, almost. As we walked past we would hear them calling out, 'Shaloni! Clara! Cynthia!' priding themselves that they could differentiate between the three of us. One lady said to Claire and me, 'Is Shaloni your mother?' pointing to Sharron. Poor Sharron was mortally offended, especially as she was the youngest.

Early one morning at around 5.00 a.m. I heard the sound of wailing coming from one of the nearby houses. The noise increased and people ran past our house, crying hysterically. We guessed that someone had died. Later we discovered it was the young man who had served us in the shop just the day before. He was only twenty-one and seemed bright and breezy. He spoke excellent English and I nearly stopped to share the gospel with him, but it was getting dark, so we left the shop and walked home. I didn't blame myself, but it made me realise the urgency for us to witness to the people we were meeting.

We often sat and talked to Bupe's oldest daughter, Chola, and Jones, her husband, playing with the younger children and the guinea-pigs. One time, there was a terrible bang. 'What's that?' I asked Jones.

'Oh, the roof of that house has fallen in,' he replied nonchalantly, as if it was an everyday occurrence.

'Was there anyone in there?' I asked quickly.

'No, they moved out some time ago,' he assured me. 'It was an old house.'

At that, we rolled about laughing. How extraordinary! It was Jones' attitude which made us laugh all the more.

We became accustomed to village life and enjoyed the time to read, write, pray and laugh together. Sometimes we went to see if 'Mrs Fritter' had cooked any deep-fried dough bread. We would walk to the local market to buy roasted ground-nuts, cassava and bananas, which was our usual supper. They had some interesting wild fruits which we often snacked on. One day, Claire was longing for a pineapple, a scarcity in our area. In fact the main market in the Boma, the centre of Kawambwa, often had very little food for sale.

'God said we could ask anything in Jesus' name and it would be done for us,' Claire reasoned, so she asked God for the seemingly impossible – a pineapple. The next day, on one of the rickety wooden market shelves, sat two small pineapples.

After washing my clothes by the outside tap at the Centre, I noticed that Isobel looked rather depressed. 'How are you doing? Is everything OK?' I inquired.

'Well, not really,' she said with a thoughtful expression. 'If I share it with you, I think you'll understand,' she began. 'There's a man who keeps transporting himself into my room using witchcraft and he sleeps with his arm around my waist. He's come three times now.'

'Is he tall, with a wide face and a moustache?' I asked.

'Yes,' she answered. 'How did you know?'

'I saw him one night when we were all sleeping in that room,' I told her. 'I woke up out of a deep sleep and there he was sitting cross-legged beside you. He looked over at me and the girls. I was so exhausted I just fell back to sleep,' I explained. I had seen the man with my physical eyes, there in our room. 'Isobel, you don't have to put up with that,' I told her. 'We have authority through Jesus Christ. He said that whatever we bind on earth will be bound in heaven. Let's pray right now and put a stop to that nonsense.'

We prayed together. 'Father, in the name of Jesus we come to You. You are the Almighty God, Ruler over the nations, Lord over everything. You are Lord over Kawambwa. In Jesus' name, we bind all powers of witchcraft; they can no longer disturb Isobel. Lord, let Your peace, Your love and Your presence protect her. Thank You, because we believe this is done. Amen!'

The matter was settled and Isobel never had that problem again. A while later I saw a man walking in the street who looked just like the one I saw that night. He completely – almost defiantly – ignored me.

The time came for us to go on another mission. Mark Kaoma went ahead to make arrangements. We waited at the roadside for a vehicle to take us to Nchelenge. A cross-eyed woman wearing a brightly coloured headscarf walked straight towards me. I recognised her from one of the potentially scary night-time encounters when her face had appeared before my closed eyes. By-passing Sharron and Claire, she put her face three inches from mine and wagged her finger at me. Almost instinctively, the words came out of my mouth: 'God bless you!' Immediately, she turned around and fled as rapidly as she had come. I guessed she had wanted to put a curse on me; Jesus said that we should bless those who curse us, so I acted on His word.

The first vehicle to arrive was driven by a drunk man. Rather than take it, we waited and eventually a public transport Land Rover arrived. It picked people up as they waited by the roadside and stopped when they needed to be dropped off. After an hour of travelling, Sharron asked if she could drive. 'Do you know how to?' the men asked in amazement. We assured them that she was quite capable and Sharron leapt into the driver's seat and drove off, turning the steering wheel constantly in order to go straight. Ahead, a woman sat by the roadside, waiting for a lift, with her possessions wrapped in a sheet. Sharron slammed her foot on the brakes, but nothing happened. The driver explained that they had to be pumped. We whizzed past the woman, who stared angrily at us, waving her hands. Eventually the vehicle came to a halt fifty metres down the road. Sharron reversed back, exclaiming with wide eyes, 'This thing doesn't have brakes!' All the Zambians laughed.

Finally we arrived in Nchelenge and met the pastors and a Zambian called Moses. Moses was married to a Danish lady called Jolanda, and they had three beautiful children. We stayed in their home which had electricity, running water and a toilet one could sit on. It seemed so luxurious. We even ate peanut butter and jam!

We went to an open space for the crusade. A crowd gathered around us as the news spread that some white people had come to visit. I preached above the hum of the crowd with Mark Kaoma interpreting. A minute into the message, silence fell on the people. I told the story from the Bible about the paralytic who was lowered through the roof where Jesus was teaching. I emphasised the forgiveness of sins, plus healing.

'Jesus is ready to heal you now!' I declared. The crowd laughed in disbelief. 'You wait,' I said. 'Some of you will find the sick people you left at home walking around, strong and completely healed.' The following day two people told me that God had done exactly that.

After the preaching one night, a little girl of about nine years old was brought to us for prayer. She had been partially deaf since birth and could not speak properly. Sharron laid hands on her and prayed. The girl fell down on to the dusty ground and got up completely healed. This testimony quickly circulated throughout the village and opened people to the gospel. Had we been able to stay there longer, we would have reaped a greater harvest of souls.

One afternoon, the whole church walked through the market-place to the lakeside singing Bemba praise songs. Crowds of inquisitive people followed us. The pastor baptised a few new believers and then we spoke. Sharron prayed for two girls to receive the Holy Spirit. The moment she removed her hands from their heads, they fell down as if dead in front of everyone. One girl rolled around in the sand and was delivered from a demon; the other one woke up speaking in tongues, although there had been no mention of this gift in our teaching sessions.

I spoke to her as we walked back to the pastor's house. She was completely overwhelmed and told me, 'I have never experienced the power of God in my life like this before.' She wondered what the special language was and I reassured her with a short explanation from the Bible. She was from a Catholic family Sharron had visited the previous day during the door-to-door evangelism. The whole household and neighbourhood had gathered to hear the Word of God and several prayed the prayer of salvation. The young lady explained, 'Recently I was very ill with cholera and I actually died. But somehow I came back to life. I realised I had to put things right with God, but I didn't know how to do this. When Sharron knocked on our door and shared the good news of Jesus Christ with us, I knew God was answering me.'

On Sunday we preached in different churches in the town and Sharron came back excited. As she had read the opening scripture, an awesome hush had settled upon the people and she wondered why. Afterwards she met the pastor, who had tears streaming down his cheeks.

'You don't know, do you?' he said to Sharron.

'Know what?' she asked, somewhat bemused.

'Three weeks ago my wife got up to preach and read the same scripture you used. But before preaching she collapsed and died a few minutes later. You preached the sermon we never got to hear,' he told her.

For the whole week we were kept busy with teaching sessions and house meetings. We prayed with the

Christians and the pastors before leaving. Moses laughed at us getting into the back of the open pick-up. 'I don't believe you!' he said when we described our house and lifestyle. 'I'll have to come and see for myself, and I'll bring some reed mats for your floors,' he promised.

Our lift took us halfway to Kawambwa and we jumped off at a junction, watching the pick-up disappearing into the distance. We lay on some mats under a tree and waited for any vehicle that might pass. We were exhausted. I relaxed, resting my head on my bag, looking up at the tall trees, admiring the freshness of the green leaves and listening to the birds. My mind went back to the past week. I was grateful to God for the way He had broken through. Many lives had been touched by His love and power. The Holy Spirit whispered encouraging words to me and my heart soared in worship of our wonderful God.

Several hours later, when still no vehicle had passed, a nurse from a nearby clinic invited us in to eat *nshima*, spicy beef and spinach. That was such a blessing. Boy, were we hungry! Eventually we heard the sound of a vehicle. We looked up in hope, happy to discover that it was going in the direction we needed. Mark ran out on to the road and waved for the driver to stop. We grabbed our bags and jumped in the back, squeezing up among the people, the live chickens and the sacks of maize flour. A woman breast-feeding her baby looked up inquisitively, as if to ask what three white ladies were doing in the middle of nowhere with no vehicle. We climbed into the pick-up, breathing a sigh of relief and giving thanks to God. If no vehicle had come we probably would have spent the night sleeping on the floor of the clinic.

On reaching Kawambwa, Chanda jumped out of the vehicle to stop a fist-fight which was erupting on the street. We went to the Centre to see Bupe's wife Vera and the children. Everything at home was fine, apart from the fact that Fled, the chicken, had died of diarrhoea and had been eaten. Mummy guinea-pig had given birth prematurely to three babies who all died, although she survived. I think the village children had enjoyed chasing them and it was all too much for poor Mummy *mpanya*.

One afternoon we went to minister in Kawambwa Boys' Secondary School. As we arrived inside the school grounds, people were running everywhere. 'What's happening?' I asked a young man.

'One of the teachers has just died,' he told me. We walked towards the home where a crowd had gathered. 'Maybe he hasn't died and Sharron can possibly help with her nursing skills,' I thought. As we drew nearer, we heard the forced wailing. Someone explained that he had been drinking the strong local brew for some years and his body had just packed up. We watched as a group of men bundled him into the back of a pick-up. I couldn't believe he was actually dead. This was the first time I had ever seen a dead body.

Sharron and I looked at each other wondering what the Lord was telling us to do.

'What do you sense, Sharron?' I asked.

After a few seconds she replied, 'I don't know.'

Soon they drove off with the body and we were left standing there dazed.

Our thoughts were interrupted by a small boy of about three years of age standing alone, howling, tears streaming down his face. No one was taking any notice of him. He was the son of the teacher. I went and hugged him and we showed love to the other children. What else could we do? As we walked away from the scene, we were moved.

'Did we miss it – or what?' I asked the others. What

would Jesus have done? I was concerned because, before we arrived in Zambia, Timothy had a dream in which God used us to raise the dead. 'Lord, if we've missed it, please forgive us,' I prayed out loud.

We walked to the schoolroom where the meeting was to take place and were taken by surprise by what God did. The Holy Spirit invaded that classroom and all we could do was worship the Lamb of God.

The next morning, back at the house, all was quiet and settled. There had been a few storms and plenty of rain. The skies became the most awesome colour before it rained and lightning frequently flashed around the sky. 'What's that?' said Claire. A low humming sound could be heard in the distance, gradually getting louder. 'It sounds like a vehicle, but it can't be!' The path to our house was only wide enough for one person to walk down. We rushed outside and saw a car coming right up to our house. It was Timothy! We went wild with excitement. The car stopped and Timothy got out, beaming as usual. We all embraced him.

'You're so thin, Timothy. What's been going on?'

'I couldn't come two weeks ago when you were expecting me because I had no money for the bus fare. Then I got malaria and when I recovered Pastor Charles offered to bring me here in his car,' he explained. They had come with some visitors for a seminar at the Centre. Then they returned to Ndola, and we followed by public means.

It was a miracle journey from Kawambwa to Ndola. Instead of the usual two days, it took us only one. We left Kawambwa at 10.00 a.m. and arrived at Kazembe, where a bus was waiting for us. As usual we chatted to the people around us, telling them about the love of God.

'How do I get this letter to the pastor in Lukwesa?' Sharron asked a passenger.

'Throw it out of the window,' she was advised. The bus hurtled past the village and the envelope fluttered and swirled down on to the road. A boy ran to pick it up.

'I hope he can read,' I commented.

'Lord, let him pass it to the right people,' Sharron prayed.

At Mansa, a kind Christian brother found a public transport Land Rover to take us on the 'short-cut' route through Zaïre. This place had a reputation for being dangerous. We had heard stories of vehicles being stopped at gunpoint so that the passengers could be relieved of their watches, wallets and other possessions before they were released to continue the journey. One of our Indian friends travelled alone on this route and was stopped by a soldier, shot dead and his body thrown by the roadside. The soldier drove the vehicle, abandoning it when it ran out of fuel. When our friend's father realised his son had not succeeded in his journey, he searched the route and found his son's body and the abandoned vehicle some miles further.

We crossed the Luapula river by tug and went through Zaïre for two hours on rough roads, praying as we travelled, finally crossing the border back into Zambia. We arrived in Kitwe and went to the police station, where we knew we could find a phone to call Timothy's wife, Kunda. We couldn't get through by telephone, and as it was getting dark we assumed we would have to stay in that town and travel in the morning. However, as we passed the market-place we saw a pick-up just leaving for Ndola. We climbed in and wrapped *gitenges* around us as protection from the cold wind. The driver only charged us 500 kwacha and took us all the way to Timothy's house instead of dropping us in town, for which we were very grateful. We arrived at 10.30 p.m. just as Charles, Timothy and Kunda pulled up in the car. They were utterly amazed that the two-day journey had taken only one day. It was nothing short of a miracle. 'We made it on Claire's faith,' Sharron said. Claire had specifically prayed for a one-day journey. We slept at Pastor Charles' house for one night – Sharron, Claire and I together in a double bed!

Later we stayed with a lovely lady called Jenny. We ate in different people's homes and ministered in the lunch-time fellowships and in Charles' church each evening. God was working, saving and healing people. We enjoyed swimming at the New Savoy Hotel pool. One day, while relaxing by the pool, I looked up from my book and saw, arriving at the hotel, the same American missionaries I had met with Jan the previous year. Amazed, I went over to speak to them. They had been relocated to a different village in Zaïre and had once again had to flee for their lives by plane. 'God wants us in Zaïre, so Zaïre it is. We'll have to go back, even if it's to yet another place,' they affirmed.

Claire returned to England and Sharron and I prepared for the next mission. We needed money for transport, as we had nothing left. On Sunday, I preached in Charles' church. Many cried as they were touched by God's presence. I spoke about God's grace shown in Jesus, and some were born again and others healed. They took up an offering for me in gratitude to God, and in addition one man who had been touched by the Lord took me to his home afterwards. 'God told me to give you 20,000 kwacha [about £40]. Don't tell my wife,' he said, handing me an envelope. She was not a believer and would not appreciate him giving the money away. It was a lot in Zambian terms, equivalent to two months' wages for a teacher at that time. I was so blessed. God had provided for us once again. It was just enough to cover our bus fare.

Sharron, Chala and I set off for a small, remote place called Masansa in Mkushi district. The journey took almost the whole day, but we arrived in time to go for a walk along a mud track and admire the beautiful sunset. In the mornings we rested and prayed. Each afternoon we walked six kilometres to a remote church. The tiny building was made of mud and had a thatched roof, with quaint rows of 'benches' made of dried mud. The pastor had invited Timothy to lead a revival there, so he sent us in his place. They sure needed a revival! On the first day when we arrived at the church, there was no one around, so someone went out to the fields where people were digging and shouted to them, calling them for the meeting. They hurriedly washed and changed their clothes, and we began.

I sensed that few people were born again, so my first message was the gospel. I was so grateful to God when almost the whole congregation responded, especially when I saw the beautiful, old, wrinkled ladies who had known such hardship. They were about to depart without knowing the One who could save their souls from hell. It brought tears to my eyes when they invited Jesus to be Lord of their lives. Their smiling faces reflected the new-found peace and love of God. How thankful I was that they had been born again before it was too late. 'O God, send out more workers into the harvest field,' my heart cried.

On another occasion, Chala brought his guitar to that small mud church. We sang songs in harmony, both in English and in Bemba. The glory of God came down, but many did not understand what was happening. We continued to sing and enjoy God's presence. It was a wonderful time.

After each meeting all the people queued outside,

singing and shaking hands with everyone. These were often the most precious times of the whole meeting and I sometimes wished we could start all over again. We walked back each day, escorted by as many as ten people. Arriving at Masansa we went immediately into the next meeting. It was good that I was accustomed to 'prayer-walking'. One day we met a woman digging in her field. She waved to us and motioned with her hand, pointing heavenwards, one hand placed on her chest and then on her leg. While we prayed for her healing, she stared up into the sky and shouted something in Bemba. Apparently she had seen angels coming to help her.

After a week, we went to Lusaka. We wanted to visit a game park and stay in one of the lodges before flying back to England. As we entered a booking office in town, the man sitting behind the desk saw us and his eyes rolled right back in his head. I stood there, inwardly binding all evil powers. We walked out quickly after getting the information we needed.

'That was weird,' said Sharron.

'Yeah,' I agreed. 'I expect it was witchcraft. Praise God for the blood of Jesus!'

The next day, we caught a bus without knowing exactly where to get the next vehicle to take us to the lodge. Once it became dark, the bus driver refused to go further than a certain small town. One of the men we were travelling with offered to help us find a guest house. We booked our rooms but they didn't serve food there. Tired and hungry, we agreed to go with this man to get something to eat. Most people in Zambia are very helpful to foreigners, but with this man I felt rather uneasy. He took us to a bar and insisted on buying us a bottle of wine which I didn't want to drink. We had not eaten all day, and as Christians in Zambia do not drink alcohol, I knew it would seem strange if we drank and then tried to witness to the people. We insisted that we should be taken back to the guest house.

Sharron and I lay on the over-used mattress, trying to sleep despite the loud music outside. I slept for a couple of hours, and then went on to the balcony for some fresh air. Rows and rows of people were sleeping with their luggage in the terrace of the next building. Sharron had not slept properly either and came out to look.

In the morning, we both felt we should leave that place, abandon the whole idea and go back to Isobel's relatives in Lusaka. We caught the early bus.

'It's a strange thing,' Sharron told me. 'This morning I was reading in Isaiah and came across a verse which said – '

'Don't tell me,' I interrupted, 'Flee for safety, run for your lives.'

'You mean, God gave you that one as well? Praise Him for His protection over us!'

Back in Lusaka, we spent time with Isobel, thanking God for everything He had done in the past three months and remembering the people whose lives He had touched. With hearts full of love and praise to God we sang the Bemba song, '*Tulemi totela . . . Takwaba ulinga imwe*' (We are grateful/thankful. There is no one like You, Lord)'.

We spent our last day at a hotel swimming-pool. In the afternoon we were met by a group of people. Isobel's son Denis had been born again in our mission to Lukwesa and we had seen him at Kawambwa Boys' School where he was studying. One of the young men there had been discipling Denis, who changed dramatically. His mother, who had previously been concerned by his rebellious behaviour, was delighted. As we sat round the pool, Denis looked up, his sincere eyes searching me. 'I have a question,' he told me.

206

'Go ahead,' I said, wondering what was coming next.

'Do you think I could be baptised here?'

Sharron and I looked at each other. 'Well, why not?' we agreed. Sharron took him through the scriptures in his new Bible before getting into the water. What a privilege it was to baptise him on our last day in Zambia. One more life had been transformed by the power of the Almighty God.

As we descended through the rain clouds at Heathrow, I thought to myself, 'Who could imagine what we have just been through? Will people read the story on our faces, or will they not really be interested?' Back in England, we soon became busy with separate lives. I met Sharron some weeks later.

'Anthea?' she said thoughtfully. 'That did all happen, didn't it? That deaf girl was really healed, we did really see all those miracles, didn't we?'

'Yep, it all happened,' I replied. 'God did it all.'

In May 1994 Timothy came to England. I was pleased to meet up with him and to hear news from Zambia. The witchdoctor who had received the Holy Spirit in Lukwesa was doing well and the church in his village was growing. Timothy told me that there were seven large villages in Luapula district with not even a single church. His vision was to plant churches in those places and he was eager for me to come back to Zambia. 'I've just planned a mission to Kenya and Uganda. Let's see how God works things out,' I told him.

I drove him to Heathrow Airport and we had plenty of time to talk while stuck in the traffic jam on the M25. We prayed together in the airport and he hugged me. 'I'm proud of you!' he said with a smile, before disappearing behind the doors.

It came as a shock to receive the news that Timothy died from a sudden illness in early 1995. He was still in his thirties, leaving behind his wife and three young daughters.

12

Times of Refreshing

We don't just want to see fruit; we want to see God

July 1994 found me in Kampala, having completed a fruitful month's ministry in Kenya with a team from England. The East and Central African Christian Leaders' conference organised by Robert Kayanja was once again accompanied by great signs and wonders and a powerful move of the Holy Spirit which affected my life profoundly. The members of my brother's band, No Bad Thing, had left their jobs for a year to devote themselves to spreading the gospel in Africa and Eastern

Europe. I joined them in Uganda.

We were given T-shirts advertising a crusade in Kampala which read, 'Come and see what brings joy in the city.' About fifty of us distributed leaflets in the streets. It poured with rain. I waited for two and a half hours at the taxi park. Taxis were returning to town, struggling through roads which had become orange rivers. Passengers accumulated until there was a crowd of about two hundred. Finally a taxi for Makindye came. People wrestled to get in the side door. Someone opened the back and two people climbed in. I weighed up the situation and then followed, scrambling over the back seat. The Ugandans were shocked to see me there, thinking white people were too dignified to do such a thing. I greeted them all in Luganda, announced the crusade and preached to those in the back.

Despite the terrible rain, the crusade was a great success. Thousands of people flocked to the Clock Tower Grounds, many standing ankle-deep in water to listen to the preaching. Members of the band climbed up to cover the speakers with plastic sheeting.

This was surely a miracle crusade. On the first day the Lord healed a man who had been unable to stand up for two years because of the epilepsy he'd had for twenty years. Another man had no eardrum and heard for the first time in twenty-eight years. God performed instant surgery on a woman's stomach tumour which had been there for ten years. One man came straight from the hospital, his stomach distended because of water on the lung. He held up his X-rays for the people to see, while showing off his new streamlined figure. He had suffered for eight years. Others clambered on to the platform to give glory to God. A woman who had received partial healing of a goitre came on the stage. Robert laid hands on her, and the people near the platform screamed as the goitre disappeared in front of their eyes. Four cripples also received their healing and walked up and down the stage carrying their crutches above their heads. The name of Jesus was praised at full volume and with complete energy.

On the second day Robert had a word of knowledge. 'There's someone at the back who has been pressurised to join a gang involved in killing people. God knows that you didn't want to get into it. But if you don't repent, within seven days you'll be dead. Walk right now to the front. We will not involve the police in this. Come forward now.' Robert kept quiet for several seconds. 'Holy Spirit, take control. Holy Spirit, take control,' he said slowly.

A man pressed through the crowd. People stepped aside in silence to make way for him. Eventually he reached the stage, prayed a prayer of repentance, surrendering his life to Jesus, and was delivered. The fear of God came on everyone.

Next Robert called people forward who had been dedicated to Satan from birth. They were all set free by the power of Jesus Christ. Many others promised to follow Jesus for the rest of their lives.

Our next two weeks were spent in Jinja. Johnson had organised evangelism for us. We set up a temporary stage for an open-air crusade in a market-place in the town centre. Adi's van had been shipped to Uganda via Mombasa and carried the team and the music equipment. His wife Justine had learnt some of the local songs. Her powerful voice resounded throughout the town through the PA system, attracting a crowd. Many of us shared testimonies and people stopped to listen to a message lasting as long as thirty minutes. People responded and names were given to the local church leaders. We packed up the equipment and drove to the next site in a village outside Jinja. Although no posters had been used for publicity, a crowd of at least a thousand people came. After gathering a harvest of souls, we packed up our things once again, this time in the semi-dark, and drove to a boys' boarding school on the top of a hill. When they heard the music they ran into the hall. The gospel was shared and a hundred and fifty eager boys raced to the front to give their lives to Jesus. I met one of the new converts in a taxi five weeks later. 'All the new believers come to the Scripture Union. God is moving powerfully,' he told me. The response in other schools was tremendous.

After this we set off for Tanzania by ferry across Lake Victoria. A crane lifted the van on to the boat and we travelled through the night for fifteen hours. The breeze was cool and the still waters glistened in the moonlight. I found a private place to pray under the stars. I had such a sense of adventure and an expectation that God would do immeasurably more than all I could ask or imagine, according to His power at work within me. 'Yes, Lord, work within me,' was my prayer.

In Mwanza, a kind Ugandan businessman, whom we nicknamed Broilers, put us up in his house, borrowing furniture from the local pastors. All the band's money had been used to release the music equipment through customs. Fortunately, God had taught the Christians in that area to give. Broilers organised a group of women to cook for us and paid for our food during our two-week stay.

The house was on the sandy shore of Lake Victoria near a trading centre where fish were sold. The heat was almost unbearable and I often woke up in the night and had a cold shower and prayed. After a few days we were joined by Godfrey and Fiona Mukasa, their two children and Johnson Musegula.

The drummer of No Bad Thing was a young man called Steve who had a great sense of humour and a desire to seek God and serve Him wholeheartedly. In the mornings Steve and I often explored the large rocky area near the house where we stayed, splitting off to pray and worship the Lord for two or three hours. Then we swam in the lake and returned for lunch. By mid-afternoon we had already set up the equipment for the crusade, which took place every day for two weeks. I preached in a lunch-time fellowship in town and at a church on the Sunday.

Towards the end of the crusade a well-known apostle who had planted several churches throughout Tanzania arrived to preach. The crowd went wild. Pastor Maboya was tall and well built, full of confidence and joy. God used him in instant healings. 'Receive a TOUCH from God!' he shouted and then let out a deep hearty laugh. 'Single touch, double manifestation!' he often said. There was great rejoicing after the miracles and conversions each evening. Maboya often requested our song, 'Mighty, mighty Saviour!'

One time, he called all the children under the age of five to the front, about four hundred in all. 'Close your eyes. Jesus is going to bless you,' he told them. He blew down the mike and they fell like dominoes on to the grass. Everybody watched in amazement. Not one child was left standing. After a five-second silence, I heard little voices laughing as the children struggled to their feet.

We went to a place outside Mwanza where many had never heard the name of Jesus. Everything we told them was new. After the preaching, some of us prayed for the sick at the side of the stage. I was quietly grateful when God healed a man who had been blind for a year. It was an encouraging sign of better things yet to come.

Johnson preached in the church where I had ministered

on Sunday. Without any prior discussion, he used the same scriptures and preached the same message about the Holy Spirit. While he was speaking, the Holy Spirit came and almost everyone in the church fell to the floor. People were quiet afterwards, knowing that God had commissioned them and equipped them for a great task up ahead.

Maboya invited us to his next crusade in Arusha, 826 kilometres from Mwanza. Adrian set off with the rest of the group, arriving twenty-four hours and several punctures later. Johnson and I took public transport, travelling through the dusty plains of the Serengeti Game Park. I prayed for the Lord to send the animals near the road as we passed. We saw miles of zebras, wildebeests and various types of deer, as well as a leopard, a hyaena, giraffes, ostriches, a lion and an elephant. We travelled through a mountainous area and past groups of Masai sitting together, having some kind of tribal debate. There were very few kilometres of tarmac road on this route. After fifteen hours of being bathed in different coloured dust, bumping around in a fast moving bus, we arrived in Arusha. But no one came to collect us from the drop-off point. As it was late, we found a guest house and prayed that somehow, in that large town, we would meet up with the others.

In the morning, we ate chicken and chips in a restaurant.

'There they are!' said Johnson, as Adi's van pulled up and parked across the road from us. We ran out of the restaurant in excitement. God truly is the Good Shepherd. They had stopped to find a market for Justine to buy some shoe polish. We went to the apartment where they had been recovering from the journey. It was plush, with white tiles on the floors. Downstairs was the president's suite and we were given his chef to cook for us. A view of

Mount Meru confronted us from the balcony. The temperature was much cooler than in Mwanza.

Due to persecution from various churches in the town, it seemed as if the crusade would be unable to take place. We persevered in prayer and the people in authority who had been persuaded to block our ministry changed their mind. We had a successful crusade meeting in a rough market-place.

I met an interesting man who had been born again a year ago in one of Maboya's crusades. He now wore his hair short, but used to be a Rastafarian with dreadlocks down to his waist. He had lived with a witchdoctor, and his drug business had made him very wealthy. When he heard the good news about Jesus, he had brought sacks of marijuana and cocaine to be destroyed openly at the crusade. 'Now my whole family and all my old customers and workmates have been saved.' He started mining tanzanite, the precious stone found only in Tanzania, and became an elder of the church.

He told me of a time when he went with Pastor Maboya to preach in a village, travelling by motorbike. Stretching across a chasm was a bridge. They discovered too late that it stopped halfway and were hurled down into the valley, somehow landing uninjured. As they sat among the pieces of the ruined motorbike they discovered they were not alone. They were surrounded by lions. They sat quietly, knowing there was nothing they could do, and the Lord sent a buffalo which frightened the lions away.

Another time, Maboya was sleeping in a temporary shelter in the bush. He wrapped the blanket tighter round him to eliminate what he thought was a draught, but it seemed to make no difference. He was alarmed to discover he was lying next to a large python. He lay rigid without moving until 10.00 in the morning, hoping the snake would go of its own accord. Eventually, he gained courage and jumped up suddenly, throwing himself against the reed door, shouting, 'Jesus!' Looking back, he saw that the snake was dead.

The band returned to Uganda, and Johnson and I stayed in Tanzania. We preached in the church in Arusha. In the middle of Johnson's message he turned to the pastor and said, 'Whoever is opposing you will not succeed!' I wondered what he was discerning in the spirit. The next day, we travelled by Land Rover over dusty roads to the mining village of Mirirani, closely followed by a lady. 'I have a message for you,' she said, opening up a folded piece of paper. She then told us the story.

'About a month ago, a man came to Arusha saying he was a refugee from Burundi. A member of our church took him in. But now we've found out that he's a satanic agent, part of a group who have destroyed three major Christian ministries in Tanzania. He was planted in our church to stop the work of God.

'Last night, he walked to the pastor's house intending to kill him. But in the place where the house should have been, there was nothing. Three times he retraced his steps and the house could not be found, so he returned home bewildered. At the gate he was confronted by an angel with a sword. He fell on his face. The angel told him, "If you don't repent, you're dead!" He cried out for mercy, and that evening he went back and found the pastor's house and confessed what he'd been doing. The pastor laid hands on him and he fell down as if dead. But they threw water on his face and revived him.

'This morning, the whole church was called together and the man confessed and repented. He pointed out the main people in the congregation who had been speaking against the pastor, and several others who had suffered misfortunes and sicknesses through the demons he had sent for those specific purposes. People began to cry and many repented openly, asking the pastor to forgive them for believing and spreading the accusations.' The Lord brought healing to the church and the work of God was strengthened.

In Mirirani, people of different tribes came together to mine precious stones. The pastor of the newly started church pointed to a young lad of seventeen who whizzed past us on a motorbike. 'You see that young man? He owns five houses.' Looking at the sandy soil and the temporary shelters where people lived it was hard to believe they were prospering. Many people used witchcraft to locate the tanzanite. We prayed that God would supernaturally show the Christians where to mine.

The power of God moved in the church meetings. Four witchdoctors came to see what was going on, but when the Holy Spirit was let loose they could no longer stay.

When we were not preaching, streams of people came to the house.

'Can you pray for my baby who's sick?'

'I want you to stand with me for my husband's salvation.'

'I'm oppressed by bad dreams.'

Maybe this was how Jesus felt, when everyone wanted to touch Him.

We left the mining village loaded with gifts: clothes, material and enough money for us to fly back to Mwanza from Kilimanjaro Airport. We travelled by boat to Uganda.

Many missions followed, as I distributed the Kingdom Faith teaching course which Alfred Kahwa and I had translated into Luganda. I gave cassettes and worksheets to pastors, travelling to many different towns. The anointing in my life had increased and many times the

Holy Spirit would invade the meetings, doing the impossible and meeting people's needs. God did everything I had desired Him to do. It was a great time of walking close to Jesus. His love held my heart firm.

There were many challenges. From June to December 1994, the longest period I slept consecutively in the same bed was ten nights. I fought sickness in Masindi and God took over in one meeting; we searched for the right church beyond Ibanda and ended up ministering in a different one. I encountered a poisonous snake in the pit latrine at Nawampendo, and once Steve put his foot in his shoe only to find a frog inside. Another time, while I was preaching on the fight of faith, an insect flew into my face and latched its pincers on to my bottom lip. I pulled it off and continued preaching.

Once I acquired some fleas from a dirty blanket and carried them with me to five different places. I used sprays and powder which should have destroyed them. They nearly drove me crazy, jumping about in my dress in the evenings. At night I could not sleep because of constant itching. I counted forty-eight bites on my left hand alone. I had prayed before but it was only when I seriously took authority in the name of Jesus Christ and refused 'no' for an answer, that they left me.

During my second night in Mirirani, some wretched bedbugs discovered my whereabouts and bit me constantly. Great stinging welts came up on my skin. My interpreter, Christine, felt sorry for me. She moved to the floor and let me sleep in her bed, but although I pulled my sleeping bag sheet tightly round my neck, within two minutes I was bitten again. I grabbed my torch and crushed five bedbugs but it was no use. They kept biting. I gave up and went outside to pray. I insisted on preaching during the day. Desperate for rest, I lay on the bed after lunch. But the bedbugs soon tracked me down. For two days and nights, I had no sleep, but continued to minister. On the third night, I swapped rooms with Johnson who prayed over the bed, pleading the protection of the blood of Jesus, and I slept soundly.

In one place, a man tried to throw a boulder at me outside the church, just before a wonderful move of God's love. Then there was the time when another minister labelled me a false teacher in front of a thousand people and caused confusion with his warped teachings. He later begged me for forgiveness for letting the devil use his mouth.

For several weeks, I suffered under harsh words from someone who turned against me. 'Lord, Your Word says that I must love my enemies, so I definitely need to love this brother in Christ. Please give me Your love,' I prayed, through my tears. I wasn't aware that God was answering my prayer until someone told me, 'We are really seeing the heart of Jesus.'

There are other stories of how Jesus healed precious people, like the man I met in the street who thought I was a doctor. 'Excuse me, excuse me madam,' he shouted across the road, running after me. 'Can you help me?' I lent him my ears.

'My name is David. I was travelling back from my wife's funeral when I had an epileptic fit on the taxi. I woke up in a hospital in Kampala and my bag and my money had disappeared. Can you give me some money so I can pay my hospital fees and go home?'

My eyes studied him carefully. I had heard similar stories which had proved to be untrue. However, the scar on his forehead acted as a witness and his sincere attitude appealed to my kindness.

'I can't give you much money,' I told him, 'but Jesus

can heal you if you put your faith in Him.' The man promptly bowed his head while we prayed there in the street. The power of God surged through my arm, nearly knocking him over. 'That's Jesus!' I told him.

Three months later, he came to see me. 'I'm like a newborn baby. I have not had a fit for all these months. I've been reading my Bible and my life now belongs to God. I've been telling people what He has done for me.' All his life, he had been treated as an outcast. He had suffered with epilepsy since birth and had never held a job for more than a month. Within a few weeks of his healing, he was accepted at a college where he acquired some skills and started a good job using his knowledge of insecticides.

Travelling back from one mission, squeezed in a taxi, I told the Lord, 'I need a break.'

'Burundi,' was His answer. And back in Kampala I found a letter from the Whites inviting me to visit and a cheque which was enough to cover the flight.

Two weeks later I returned to Uganda. Agnes Kabatesi, an ex-Roffey student who had started a work with orphan children, invited me to stay in her house, together with Claire Hollis who had come to visit. I had always wondered why Agnes seemed anxious I stayed with her and one day I found out. She left a letter on my bed which she had written three years before, while at Roffey Place. She had not found the courage to give it to me then. In it she described two dreams in which the Lord showed her that I would come to Uganda and that God would use her to look after me. And during the next year and a half, she certainly did, laying down her life in such loving ways. I used her house as a base and it was a haven to come back to. She fed me well, refusing to accept money offered for food, as she knew that any financial support I received was quickly used up on transport.

I have always worked on the principle that if God wants to send me anywhere, He will pay. One day, I set off for a mission in Busia with only enough money to get there. On the journey, I met two Christian ladies who gave me enough money to cover the return journey. And after the week's ministry, the pastor also paid for my taxi fare.

A similar thing happened when I was due to travel by boat to Mwanza, Tanzania. The day before, I preached at Trumpet Centre in Kampala, using my last shillings to get there. Unbeknown to them, I was believing God for the money to take me to Tanzania the next day. After the meeting, an envelope was given to me containing enough money to cover my fare. I knew this was God, as gifts were not a frequent occurrence in Uganda.

One time, Sharron came to Uganda and we travelled by boat to Mwanza, where we stayed with a lady whose husband was a Muslim. She showed us to our room and gave us beautiful fabrics as gifts. Early one morning, I lay awake on the top bunk of our bed and prayed out loud, chuckling to myself as I thought of the victory we have through Jesus Christ. Suddenly, the Holy Spirit fell on Sharron who rapidly became helpless with loud peals of laughter. After a few seconds, there was a timid knock on the door, but we were laughing too much to answer. Later in the day, I heard what had happened. The wife had come to the door and caught the Holy Spirit laughter. Entering her bedroom, her husband was also infected. 'Ho ho, ha, ha, ha! What is this spirit that has come into the house? Ha, ha! We must stop this; it could be dangerous,' said the Muslim man. He took the children to school and the people they passed in the road were also overcome with laughter. The lady was excited that her husband was a step nearer the Kingdom.

After a week of successful ministry, we stood at the port. I hadn't told Sharron that we didn't have enough money for our port tax. A church member took our passports. 'I'll work on your visas,' he told me, and the passports came back with everything stamped and paid for, including two first-class tickets. God is a good God.

Later, while in Morogoro, Tanzania, I stayed with a lady who had planted eleven churches among the Masai people. 'We started from scratch,' she told me. 'We learnt the culture and taught people biblical principles of living, eliminating any demonic ceremonies and traditions.'

I went to Masai land. Thankfully the driver had a good sense of direction as there was no road, not even a track or a path. He drove over the sandy ground, dodging the trees and shrubs. The Masai welcomed me with big hugs and prayers of blessing. They were so open and friendly. I slept on a mattress under a hot iron-sheet roof, rather than sleeping on skins in a traditional shelter. The seminar took place at a school, twenty-five minutes' journey away. I rode on the back of a loaded bicycle, one lad sitting on the cross bar, and another on the saddle. The Masai people were on fire for Jesus, grateful for their new-found freedom. I met a lovely lady, one year old in the Lord, whom God had used to raise a dead person.

I had an interest in these people and found out about their culture which was completely different from the surrounding people groups. The Masai traditions have been passed down the generations and there is a reluctance to change, as pressure from the community is so strong. Their identity is in the way they dress. The men look after the cattle, often disappearing during dry seasons to take them near water. Cows are their pride and joy. If they find one wandering somewhere, they will take it because they believe all cows on earth belong to the Masai. Everything centres around the cattle and a man's wealth is measured in the number he owns, so rather than selling one they choose to live very simply, in grass huts. Now mud huts are becoming more popular, especially with the born-again Masai. Masai are tending to settle; the ones in that area had lived in the same place since the 1950s, which was quite a record.

Men can have several wives and children, living in separate houses in one enclosure. The women don't mind the husband having other wives, in fact they are often pleased to have more help in milking cows, which is the woman's responsibility. Traditionally, she dresses in a special way for the sacred art of milking. Her many earrings and necklaces have various meanings. Some very heavy earrings are worn to protect the husband. If she takes them off, she may be accused of wanting him to die. The ladies also wear many copper rings on their arms which scar them for life, as they dig into the skin and sometimes become embedded. The 'loopy' ears are produced during a ceremony where they pierce the ear, inserting a small twig into the hole. After a few days they put in a larger stick, and later replace it by an even larger one, and then one more, until the lobe has stretched permanently. Most of their charms involve demonic powers, so deliverance normally occurs at salvation.

Once they grow spiritually, many things change. For example, traditionally when the wife cooks, she leaves the food and disappears while the husband comes to eat, as she is not allowed to see him eating. When they are both born again, they eat together. The traditional diet of a Masai is cow's blood and milk, but some now eat foods like beans and rice cooked in milk, as water is not always found in the dry areas where they live. After salvation, the husband who has many wives decides which one to stay with and tries to cater for the others. Young girls, normally given away to men at extremely young ages, remain single for longer and serve the Lord. The traditional jumping up and down on the spot to great heights has developed among the Christians into a form of praise to God, while singing a song.

Masai people are very sincere and never lie. Neither do they steal, their attitude about cows being the exception. People were amazed as they carefully turned the pages of my Bible. Books are not commonplace, although more Masai are being encouraged to become educated and study Kiswahili at school. Illiteracy is quite a barrier to overcome in spreading the gospel and their concentration span is limited. However, they accept the truth completely and have a strong fear of God. Once they realise they have been wrong, they are willing to change and they stand firm despite opposition and alienation from their Masai community. It was encouraging to be part of what God was doing among the Masai people for a few days.

13

Lord of the Islands

God specialises in the impossible

'Can I come with you to the islands?' I asked John
Mulinde. Agnes had put me in contact with 'The Apostle'
from Worldwide Trumpet Mission based in Kampala.
Apart from other activities, teams preach in remote places
where no one else wants to go. For two years he had
gathered Christians together on the islands in Lake
Victoria, strengthening them in the Word of God,
establishing them in prayer and evangelising.

On many islands there was no church. Other

denominations had tried to plant churches, often without success. Many islanders are in hiding from the police on the mainland, earning a living by fishing. The ungodliness and opposition to the work of the gospel was evident when one church was repeatedly burnt down until the thatched roof was replaced by corrugated iron sheets. As the presence of God was manifested on one island, witch-doctors were chased to another island. Then the gospel was established there and they found themselves running away to another island. Jesus said, 'But if I drive out demons by the Spirit of God, then the kingdom of God has come upon you' (Matt. 12:28).

Sharron and I had just returned from Tanzania and spent a couple of nights at Agnes' house. I remember the night before we were due to set off to visit Lubiya Island. There was a battle raging in the heavenlies, but I didn't force myself to wake up and pray because I was so tired. By the time we left to go to Jinja, I knew we didn't have the breakthrough for the mission, but I believed we would get it when we were there. Experience has shown that what God does on a mission or in a meeting often depends on how far you go in prayer beforehand. When God touches your heart and you have that awesome release of joy in His presence, you know that your prayers have been heard. The hindering forces have shifted to make room for a move of God and He does what I call a Holy Spirit take-over. That kind of ministry is effortless. God invades the place with His presence and meets the needs of the people. On this occasion, I knew we were not in that place spiritually.

We travelled to Jinja by public transport and made our way to the fishing port, riding down a very bumpy track sitting on the back seat of a *boda-boda* bicycle, our bags piled up and tied on the back of another bike. There appeared to be a disagreement about the charge and for several minutes we stopped until negotiations were completed. On arriving at the fishing port, we sat and waited for the boat to return from a fishing trip. There was a heavy downpour of rain and we huddled together in a tiny shelter, hungry and cold, squatting on our bags.

At last the boat arrived. It was an open wooden boat with an engine at the back. We avoided inhaling while two men cleaned the fish scales off and placed reed mats across the wooden planks for us to sit on. Ten of us climbed in and Sharron caught my eye and laughed. We took a photo. 'The guys back home wouldn't believe this!' we agreed. We left at 6.00 p.m., the sky already dark and cloudy. 'Surely we must be arriving soon. How long is this journey supposed to be?' I thought, after travelling for three hours. Even if someone had told me how long it was, I wouldn't have been convinced. It's difficult to assess time in Africa. Time is not an issue to many people outside Western civilisation. It's always best to listen to the Holy Spirit when arrangements are being made. You can be told to come at 5.00 but if the Holy Spirit says they won't be there until 6.00, you make sure you turn up in God's time. He understands timing, yet He is not governed by it.

The large waves crashed over the sides of the boat and the fishermen handed us a black polythene sheet to cover ourselves. A puddle formed and then ran down, soaking us. We adjusted to the idea of sitting in water. Then the engine stopped abruptly. The fishermen tried to restart it, but after several minutes they gave up, and I heard them saying, *Tugenda kusula mumazi*. Oh no! I didn't have the heart to tell Sharron immediately that we would have to spend the night on the lake. The men let down some fishing nets which they somehow rigged to make an anchor. We later discovered that a piece of wood holding the engine in place had broken in half. The engine had slipped down, becoming completely waterlogged.

The waves knocked constantly against the boat and I felt considerably sick. The idea of spending a night there sounded horrendous. I struggled against the feelings of nausea. 'Sharron.'

'Yes.'

'Pray for me.'

She did, and I felt better. But immediately after praying, she vomited over her side of the boat, and then I clambered over the young man sitting next to me and did the same. We lay down flat to reduce the swaying sensation, five of us squashed together in one small section of the boat. The man next to me was half lying on me, giving me a dead leg, but there was nowhere else he could move. Somehow he managed to fall asleep with his neck at the strangest angle. The reed mat capsized and we lay in the water like upside-down crabs, our legs in the air. Every now and again, someone struggled up to vomit, while the boat constantly thrashed about in the waves. Someone tried to bail water from the bottom of the boat, using a cut-open jerrican.

The fishermen looked around nervously, afraid of drifting into the nearby rocks. I viewed the land some distance from our boat. Swimming in that mass of swirling water would have been very dangerous. If one of us panicked and stood up, the whole boat could have easily overturned and Sharron and I were the only swimmers. Thankfully everyone remained calm.

'Aren't there any oars?' I asked.

'Any what?'

'You know,' I said, demonstrating with my hands.

The fishermen smirked, as if it would have been most unusual to have oars in a boat.

Thunder rumbled round like an angry lion stalking its prey. The lightning struck the water nearby. Heavy rain pelted deafeningly on the polythene sheets. We huddled together trying to keep warm, soaked through. Despite feeling sick, we started to sing loudly, competing with the noise of the rain.

'What would Jesus have done in this situation?' I asked myself.

There was no point making a dramatic scene, commanding the engine to start, unless I had a definite word from God. If I had acted in hope, or on my own initiative, nothing would have happened.

Sharron cried out to God, refusing every fear-inspiring thought the enemy threw at her.

'God must be waking people up in England to pray for us,' I told her. I lay there looking up into the dark sky. 'Lord, I'm here. I know You can see me clearly. I can't get out of this situation. Please do something.'

I felt the Father's reassuring arms around me. Not only was He looking down from heaven, but the Great I Am was right there with me in the boat, by His Holy Spirit. I was bathed in the presence of the One who is outside the limitations of this world. I had no worries for my life, but a calm confidence that my Saviour was at work. My thoughts focused on the people of the island and I sensed the urge to intercede for them. The battle was for the salvation of souls and for the name of Jesus to be glorified in that place.

Somehow we got through the night, praying, dozing, vomiting. Finally dawn broke. We saw a fishing boat approaching and one of our group stood up, shouting and frantically waving a piece of cloth, but we remained unnoticed. The fishermen pulled the engine cord while everyone prayed under their breath. After several splutters and coughs, the boat darted away like an unleashed dog, and after fifty minutes we reached Lubiya.

With relief we set our feet down on solid ground, walking as if drunk, still feeling the motion in our heads. The Christians ran to greet us on the shore, their faces beaming. On-lookers seemed surprised to see a *muzungu* on the island. John Mulinde walked with us to a little mud house and we told him briefly what had happened. 'We sensed you might be caught on the lake in the storm, but we didn't dare to believe it was true. We were awake most of the night praying for you,' he told us.

We crowded into the house and sang praises. John cried in gratitude to God. Tears flowed as we thanked Him for rescuing us. I had been so calm and trusting on the boat, but a previously unnoticed bubble burst in relief. We had spent fifteen hours on the water!

To dispel the swaying movement in our heads, Sharron and I lay down on a single bed behind a curtain in the mud hut. We slept soundly for a few hours, and then I went out to explore the island. I found a nearby beach and the waves crashed against me as I jumped around and swam in the refreshing water, washing off the green dye which had come out of my dress.

Walking back to the house, I met John Mulinde. 'You're preaching in the crusade tonight,' he told me. It was due to start in a few minutes. I had hoped for more time to prepare. I stood behind a large rock on the shore, the only private place I could find, looked out over the lake at the small fishing boats, and noticed another island in the distance. Worship of the Creator stirred in my heart as I began to talk to Him. I wanted the specific message for the islanders. I needed a fresh touch from Him so they would not simply hear words, but would receive the very life of God. Jesus said, 'Whoever believes in me, as the

Scripture has said, streams of living water will flow from within him' (John 7:38). As I prayed, I knew the living waters would flow on that island. The Holy Spirit prompted me to read the story of the woman caught in the act of adultery (John 8:1–11). I didn't know then that one of the main strongholds on the island was adultery and promiscuity.

At the grassy crusade ground, we sat for a few moments while the praise team sang. They were standing on a temporary stage made from wooden planks and logs. People came out of the nearby houses to enjoy the music and hear the Word of God. We were welcomed by the chief of the island who told us how much he appreciated our visit. 'Although I'm not a born-again Christian, I'm sure that we, on this island, need to hear your message. There has been much wickedness here. So you are free to preach whatever is on your hearts, even if it's a hard message.'

I climbed up the rickety ladder and stood on the stage. The people were attentive, and as I spoke the Lord's presence came through. I saw genuine conviction on their faces; at the end, several walked forward to respond to the message. Two of them were almost crying, touched by the grace and mercy of God. I laid hands on them and prayed, and the pastor took their names.

'There's a lady here who has suffered for many months with pains in her legs. Just come forward. Jesus wants to heal you,' I said. She walked slowly towards the stage. I put my hand on her head and the power of God touched her. The pain left instantly and she could walk with no problem. The next day we were greeted by her radiant face and were told the whole story. She had been bewitched and as a result suffered sharp pains in one of her legs. She spent three months in hospital on the mainland, but the doctors could do nothing for her. Jesus healed her completely and she could walk without pain.

People also brought a little boy on to the stage. He had been very badly burnt as a baby, and although he was at least three years old he had never been able to stand or walk. All his limbs were twisted up. We laid hands on him and prayed. Everybody watched eagerly, some ready to mock, as we tried to stand him up on the stage. Nothing visibly changed. I handed him back to his mother: 'Just believe Jesus. You're about to see something amazing.' After we had left the island, the miracle took place. The little boy sat on the ground beside his mother while she cooked. For the first time in his life, he stood up and started to walk. She took him around the whole island saying, 'Look what Jesus has done for my little boy.' Later she also committed her life to the Lord.

The next morning, I got up before the sun became too hot. Sharron was still asleep so I slipped out quietly and walked towards a long stretch of sandy beach which could be seen from our house. Down a narrow path wading through some thick vegetation, I nearly bumped into a man holding a knife. Shock gave way to relief as he broke into a smile. We greeted in Luganda and I walked on, my heart beating fast. 'God has not given me a spirit of fear, but a spirit of love, power and a sound mind,' I said under my breath. Eventually, I found an opening on to the beach. Something caught my eye. It was a three-foot-long lizard scuttling into the nearby bushes. I was so glad to have learnt the previous week that those creatures were harmless.

I sat down on the golden sand and looked out over the lake. The scenery was spectacular, but I closed my eyes and meditated on God's goodness. He was so close, and before I knew it, I was oblivious to my surroundings. Aware only of Him, I heard myself groaning deeply, again and again. I remembered the scripture which says, 'In the same way, the Spirit helps us in our weakness. We do not know what we ought to pray for, but the Spirit himself intercedes for us with groans that words cannot express. And he who searches our hearts knows the mind of the Spirit, because the Spirit intercedes for the saints in accordance with God's will' (Rom. 8:26–7). I knew God had achieved something. I cooled myself down by swimming in the clear water before walking back to the house. What a life!

That morning people gathered under a temporary shelter made from sacking tied to wooden poles. The mud and thatch church building was too small to accommodate the crowds who wanted to come and hear. I spoke about being a new creation. 'Once we were enemies of God but now, through Christ Jesus, we have been brought close to God. We need no longer conform to the standards of this world. We must be transformed by the renewing of our minds.' People were touched and challenged. After the teaching session, everyone stood and prayed, and the Holy Spirit came to do His work. Demons manifested and departed, and many were filled with the Holy Spirit.

In the afternoon Sharron preached. One could feel the air of expectancy. Those who needed healing came forward. There were too many to reach from the stage, so we jumped down and laid hands on them, communicating through an interpreter, checking that each one had received their healing from God before praying for the next. The praise team continued to sing. One girl was so taken over by the Holy Spirit that she fell off the stage unharmed and lay on the grass in the presence of God.

Suddenly a great shout went up near Sharron. Everyone jumped around, praising God. Sharron had prayed for a man in his thirties, deaf and dumb from birth. She told the pastor to speak to him in Luganda. Still new in faith, he refused, saying, 'No, this man cannot hear or speak.'

'But the Lord has healed him,' Sharron replied.

The pastor turned to the man and said, '*Mukama yebazibwe!* Praise the Lord!'

'*Amina!* Amen!' the man answered. He turned round swiftly to hear the ladies singing, the first sound he had ever heard. We continued to pray for men, women and children as more sick people were brought out of their houses. Many fell on to the dusty ground as demons and sicknesses were driven out by the authority of Jesus Christ, the Son of the living God. The Lord was certainly glorified!

Later in the evening seventy people shared a meal outside under the stars, telling what God had done in their lives. In the morning, we boarded the boat, loaded with gifts – two live chickens, petticoats, drinking glasses and handkerchiefs, all bought from a shop on the island. We travelled back satisfied. God had been at work and His rule was being established on the island of Lubiya.

I was excited when I heard that Mission Aviation Fellowship (MAF) had built a floatplane which could land on the water. I used it to visit two islands with my sister, Alison, who had just completed a one-year course at Roffey Place Bible College. We set off early in the morning by taxi, changing vehicles on the way to Kaazi, where the floatplane was kept.

It poured with rain, turning sections of the mud road into a fast-flowing orange river, the colour of the soil. The driver panicked at the wheel, doing several 280-degree turns in the mud. Somehow he managed to avoid trees, other cars and houses, and we were thankful that we didn't end up in one of the ditches on either side of the road.

At Kaazi, the water was too choppy for the plane to take off, and so we had to wait for some time before strapping ourselves in the plane and zooming along the water until we had lift-off. We sighted the correct island from the air, circling several times to find the best landing place, where the water was calm and free from rocks. As we descended, people rushed to the shore from all directions, excited to see us, thinking we had flown direct from England. We joined the crowds and the pilot took off, leaving us on the island. I used my small knowledge of Luganda and Kiswahili to ask where the Trumpet Mission church was. Someone thought they knew and ten people came with us, carrying our luggage. Communication was difficult and it took me a while to realise that the word for 'aeroplane' was also the name of a village on the island. They kept asking me if I was going to the plane, and I kept telling them the plane had gone. They didn't agree, because to them I was saying that the village had gone. We really laughed when we realised what had been happening.

After walking for forty minutes we came to a house belonging to a pastor. We were welcomed warmly and waited while someone ran to fetch him. They asked us if we liked to eat chicken, hoping we would stay. When the pastor arrived, we discovered this wasn't the right church and we insisted that we should go and find the people who were waiting for us, rather than minister there.

Some of the ladies offered to take us to another church. We walked down a narrow path with grass high above our heads on either side. It became dark. After three hours, we found a large church building. The pastor welcomed us. 'Now you're here, I will call the people for an overnight meeting,' he said.

Realising this was not the right place, I told them we

would not minister. We asked if they had somewhere where we could rest and sleep for the night, as we were quite tired from the journey. One of the Christian families offered to put us up. They were Kenyans. The children were fascinated with us, as we must have been the first white people they had ever seen. They kept their distance, but every so often their curiosity would bring them closer to us. If we spoke to them, they would run away, screeching and giggling.

Two plastic bowls of water were placed round the back of the house. 'Isn't this exciting?' said Ali, as we washed in the light of the moon.

'Isn't what exciting?' I asked. 'Oh, I see. This has become normal for me now. Yes, it's great, isn't it?'

We came back into the mud hut to find a mattress on the floor of the living area. This was Ali's first night of sleeping in such a house. We lay 'top-to-tail' on the single mattress. There seemed to be so many creepy crawlies in that place. I really don't mind those innocent little creatures, except if they bite or sting. Unfortunately, these ones did, and we found ourselves tossing, turning and scratching all night. At one point Ali said she thought something was nibbling her feet. I think she had been hearing too many stories of hungry rats. I put my hand out where her feet were and felt something very furry. I screamed, and poked and shoved it until it ran away. We lay there recovering from our shock.

'Hey Ali, did you notice that ginger cat in the house?' I questioned. 'It felt so soft, maybe it was that.'

After about half an hour, I was aware of something warm and furry between my head and Ali's feet. Yes, it was the ginger cat. I put my hand out to stroke it, feeling rather sorry that I had hit it so hard.

Morning finally came and I tried to convince Ali that

not all mud huts were like this one. It just happened to be her first experience. We had some milky Kenyan *chai* and set off once again to report to the local authorities before finding the Trumpet Mission people. When we found them, although we had never met before, it felt good to be with like-minded people.

'Where's the group from Kampala?' I asked.

They were supposed to have come by boat the day before us. It seemed that the programme had been changed, so we crossed by boat to another island to look for them. The water was a bit choppy but our lunch survived the journey. Arriving on the sandy shore of Sagitu Island we heard the preaching. Our white skin became a major distraction as we walked into the crusade ground. The people had been told we were coming but hadn't believed it.

There followed a busy schedule of teaching in the mornings and evenings in the church and preaching in the crusade in the afternoon. We stayed in a thatched house, fifteen of us sleeping on mattresses all over the floor, two per mattress. Some had come from Kampala, and some from other islands, including the lady from Lubiya whose leg had been healed. One night we were woken up by rain leaking through the roof. After ten minutes, it was raining as much inside as it was outside. People stumbled around blurry-eyed, gathering their belongings and stacking their mattresses in the driest corner.

'Where's Ali?' Annette inquired, and a little muffled voice answered, 'I'm in here.' Ali was keeping dry, sandwiching herself inside a folded-up mattress. Eventually the rain subsided, by which time most people were asleep in the porch outside the house, which was the driest patch. Oh, the life of a missionary!

Throughout the week, many people were saved and we

baptised forty-nine of them in the lake. The pastor was strengthened to continue in the work, despite the great cost to his own life. He was an educated man, capable of running his own business in the city. He told us his story:

'I came to visit a relative living on the island and when I shared Jesus with the people, many gave their lives to the Lord. I couldn't face the thought of leaving them to backslide, with no one to teach and care for them. In my heart I felt I should establish a church here. Many years ago I received a prophecy which I didn't believe at the time. I was told I would be a pastor. I wouldn't have chosen such a task, but it was the Lord's plan. My family thought I was crazy because I could be earning good money. But here I am.'

After a few days we returned to the original island to conduct a three-day crusade and to teach the Christians. We were taken past a wooden pole sticking out of the ground with a sign on it saying, 'Police Post'. We entered a small room containing wooden benches and a desk. It was the police station. Ali and I were questioned in the office for almost an hour.

'Why have you come to the island?' one man asked gruffly.

'We've come to preach the gospel,' I told them.

'But how do we know?' they asked, trying to intimidate us.

'You can come and hear us preaching,' I said, wondering what was the cause of their concern.

At that time, there was some unrest in one area of Uganda. When the police had heard the plane circling the island earlier on in the week, they had panicked, especially since we hadn't been found on the island immediately, having gone to Sagitu. They suspected that we had come to train rebels. Looking at my sister's innocent little face

I wondered how on earth they could come to such a conclusion. They radioed the Kampala police and then released us, by which time we had missed the first crusade meeting.

This island had a completely different atmosphere to the other one. It was quite a busy fishing port with people of different nationalities. The spiritual climate was also interesting, with many other religions and sects and loose moral standards. It was one of those rough crusades where the Holy Spirit had to come through to capture the attention of the people, or else there would be chaos! I stood on a rock with my interpreter. People gathered round. That week was a challenge and we battled in prayer. The Holy Spirit broke through in the preaching and it was satisfying to see many people openly responding to the call to repent and believe the good news. Several were instantly healed by the power of Jesus as I prayed a general prayer over the crowd.

In the second crusade meeting, the rain clouds drew threateningly near. Once the rain comes, it can drench a person in ten seconds; as soon as the wind is felt, people run to find shelter, as rain can often bring fever. Before preaching, I looked up at the clouds and asked the Lord to keep them back, and He did. One man came up to me afterwards and said, 'There are some things I don't understand.' I thought he would be asking questions about his salvation, but he told me, 'I saw a big screen between us and the rain clouds. And another strange thing – what was that transparent blue light around you when you were praying for the sick?'

'That was the power of God,' I told him.

Time came for us to leave. We looked back fondly at our friends standing on the shore as the boat took us out on to the lake again. I prayed in my heart for the Lord to

239

continue the work there and strengthen those who were serving Him. Many precious babes had entered into a whole new world and needed care and attention.

On the other island, a crowd welcomed us back and some ladies cooked a late lunch of fresh fish and rice. We were expecting the MAF pilot to come with the Jesus film, stay the night and then take us back in the morning. I started to prepare my message for the crusade when we heard the sound of the plane. We waved a piece of cloth as it flew over. When the plane landed, we were amazed to see our friend Patrick from the other island and Mathew Bridle, a member of our church in England who was staying with Mum and Dad at the Orphanage in the depths of the bush. 'What's he doing here?' I exclaimed.

The story went like this. The Kampala police had contacted MAF and a message reached my parents' house that we were stranded on an island, detained in prison, unable to be released until someone brought our passports. Mathew received the message while Mum and Dad were out. He travelled to our house in Kampala, broke down our bedroom doors to get our passports, and flew with MAF, first to one island, and then to the other. Mathew to the rescue! We had been preaching all week and knew nothing about prisons and passports.

Sadly we had to return with the plane that day. Ali boarded the plane, blinking back her tears. The islanders were equally disappointed. They had been expecting to see the Jesus film. I promised the pastor we would return in one week's time with the film. Standing on the floater of the plane, I shouted to the crowd, '*Tugenda 'komawo!* We're coming back!'

There have been other adventures on the islands and the work in the remote villages continues as I travel out from my rented house in Kampala. A few months ago, I started helping street children in the city as well as giving practical help to orphans in different parts of the country. The Word of God is being preached, bringing changes in people's lives. 'We've never heard such teaching before,' people often tell me after I have expounded basic biblical Christianity. God confirms His Word with signs and wonders, healing many who often have the choice to believe God for a miracle or die. God has been moving mightily through other ministries in Uganda, healing hundreds of people from AIDS and demonstrating that He is a God of mercy and great compassion.

My aim is to stay close to Jesus, who said, 'He who abides in me and I in him, bears much fruit; for without Me you can do nothing.' (John 15:5, NKJ). Teams continue to come to Uganda and the surrounding countries, and groups of Ugandans accompany me beyond the borders of Africa. Millions of precious people, whose souls are valuable to God, still wait to be reached with the greatest message the world will ever hear.

I Believe in Mission

(The New *I Believe* Series)

Alistair Brown

For Christians the desire that others might also believe in Christ should be natural and instinctive, says Alistair Brown. For some, that will mean sharing their faith with family, friends, colleagues and neighbours. For others, the call to the unevangelised areas of the world will be powerful.

Whether called to share our faith at home or abroad, mission is the responsibility and privilege of every Christian. Mission is commanded by God, and is necessary if people are not to be lost. Mission also requires great passion: it's not merely spiritual scalp-hunting – it means caring for the whole person's needs.

This book is a biblical and practical call to mission. Only through radical, compassionate mission can the dream of a changed world be realised.

Alistair Brown is General Director of the Baptist Missionary Society, and the author of *Near Christianity*.

0 340 69427 0

The Street Children of Brazil

Sarah de Carvalho

Her glittering career in film promotion and TV
production took her to California, Sydney and London.
But her international lifestyle and fast-lane salary gave
her no time to enjoy herself.

Through a series of remarkable events, Sarah left her
career and joined a missionary organisation in
Brazil. There she met children from the age of
seven living on the streets, taking drugs, stealing
to survive and open to prostitution and
gang warfare.

This is the remarkable true story of a life transformed.
It tells of the incredible work that Sarah de Carvalho
and her husband have founded in the Happy
Child Mission. It is a story of immense faith,
suffering and love. The children whose stories are
revealed in this exceptional book will change
the heart of
every reader.

0 340 64164 9